First World War
and Army of Occupation
War Diary
France, Belgium and Germany

3 DIVISION
7 Infantry Brigade
Duke of Edinburgh's (Wiltshire Regiment)
1st Battalion
4 August 1914 - 31 October 1915

WO95/1415/2

The Naval & Military Press Ltd
www.nmarchive.com
Published in association with The National Archives

Published by

The Naval & Military Press Ltd

Unit 10 Ridgewood Industrial Park,
Uckfield, East Sussex,
TN22 5QE England
Tel: +44 (0) 1825 749494

www.naval-military-press.com

www.nmarchive.com

This diary has been reprinted in facsimile from the original. Any imperfections are inevitably reproduced and the quality may fall short of modern type and cartographic standards.

© Crown Copyright
Images reproduced by permission of The National Archives, London, England, 2015.

Contents

Document type	Place/Title	Date From	Date To
Heading	WO95/1415 3 Div 7 Infantry Bde 1 Battn. Wiltshire Regt. August 1914-Oct 1915		
Heading	3rd Division 7th Infy Bde 1st Battalion The Wiltshire Regiment Aug-Dec 1914		
Heading	7th Brigade. 3rd Division. 1st Battalion The Wiltshire Regiment August 1914		
Heading	War Diary 1st Batt. Wiltshire Rgt. Volume I 4-31.8.14		
War Diary	Tidworth	04/08/1914	31/08/1914
Miscellaneous	App II		
Miscellaneous	Landing Return. App I	14/08/1914	14/08/1914
Heading	7th Brigade 3rd Division. 1st Battalion The Wiltshire Regiment September 1914		
Heading	1st Wiltshire Regt. Vol II with Appendices to Vol I		
War Diary		31/08/1914	02/09/1914
War Diary		31/08/1914	30/09/1914
Miscellaneous	Report on attack in the Right Section. App III	23/09/1914	23/09/1914
Diagram etc	Rough Sketch of position on Sunday 20 Sept 1914		
Miscellaneous	Messages And Signals.		
Miscellaneous	Field State. App IV		
Miscellaneous	1st Bn Wiltshire Regt. App V	25/09/1914	25/09/1914
Miscellaneous	Statement Diaries of No. 4591 Coy Quarters Master Left W. G. Lester	25/09/1914	25/09/1914
Miscellaneous	To O.C. Wiltshire Regt	25/09/1914	25/09/1914
Miscellaneous	From O.C. D Coy 1/Wiltshire Reg.	25/09/1914	25/09/1914
Miscellaneous	Statement of Diaries for Recommnding No.8765 Lane Corporal C Street		
Miscellaneous	Field State. App VI	26/09/1914	26/09/1914
Diagram etc	Outpost Position at Chassemy. App VII		
Heading	7th Brigade. 3rd Division. 1st Battalion The Wiltshire Regiment October 1914		
Heading	1st Battn. Wiltshire Rgt. Vol III 1-27.10.14		
War Diary		01/10/1914	27/10/1914
Miscellaneous	1st Bn Wiltshire Regt.		
Miscellaneous			
Heading	7th Brigade.3rd Division. 1st Battalion The Wiltshire Regiment November 1914		
Heading	7th Brigade. 1st Wiltshire Regt. Vol IV 1-30.11.14		
War Diary		01/11/1914	01/11/1914
War Diary	Locre Belgium	02/11/1914	02/11/1914
War Diary	Locre	03/11/1914	04/11/1914
War Diary	Hooge	05/11/1914	20/11/1914
War Diary	Westoutre	21/11/1914	27/11/1914
War Diary	Scherpenberg	28/11/1914	30/11/1914
Miscellaneous	Rough estimate of our wastage since the Company		
Heading	7th Brigade. 3rd Division. 1st Battalion. The Wiltshire Regiment December 1914		
Heading	7th Brigade 1st Battn. Wiltshire Regt. Vol V 1-31.12.14		
War Diary	Kemmel	01/12/1914	02/12/1914
War Diary	Westoutre	03/12/1914	05/12/1914
War Diary	Locre	06/12/1914	08/12/1914

War Diary	In Trenches near Kemmel	09/12/1914	11/12/1914
War Diary	Locre	12/12/1914	14/12/1914
War Diary	In Trenches near Kemmel	15/12/1914	18/12/1914
War Diary	Locre	19/12/1914	23/12/1914
War Diary	In Trenches near Kemmel	24/12/1914	27/12/1914
War Diary	Westoutre	28/12/1914	30/12/1914
War Diary	Locre	31/12/1914	31/12/1914
Heading	3rd Division 7th Infy Bde. 1st Battalion Wiltshire Regt. Jan-Oct 1915		
Heading	7th Inf Bde. 3rd Div. War Diary 1st Battn. The Wiltshire Regiment January 1915		
War Diary	Locre	01/01/1915	03/01/1915
War Diary	In Trenches near Kemmel	04/01/1915	07/01/1915
War Diary	Locre	08/01/1915	11/01/1915
War Diary	In Trenches near Kemmel	12/01/1915	15/01/1915
War Diary	Locre	16/01/1915	19/01/1915
War Diary	In Trenches near Kemmel	20/01/1915	23/01/1915
War Diary	Locre	24/01/1915	27/01/1915
War Diary	In Trenches near Kemmel	28/01/1915	31/01/1915
Miscellaneous	Notes on the Operations during the past month		
Heading	7th Inf. Bde. 3rd Div. War Diary 1st Battalion The Wiltshire Regiment February 1915		
War Diary	Locre	01/02/1915	04/02/1915
War Diary	In Trenches near Kemmel	05/02/1915	08/02/1915
War Diary	Locre	09/02/1915	11/02/1915
War Diary			
War Diary	In Trenches near Kemmel	17/02/1915	21/02/1915
War Diary	Locre	22/02/1915	22/02/1915
War Diary			
War Diary	In Trenches near Kemmel	28/02/1915	03/03/1915
Heading	7 Inf. Bde. 3rd Div. War Diary 1st Battalion The Wiltshire Regiment March 1915		
War Diary	In Trenches near Kemmel	01/03/1915	03/03/1915
War Diary	Locre	04/03/1915	12/03/1915
War Diary			
War Diary	Kemmel	17/03/1915	22/03/1915
War Diary	La Clyte	23/03/1915	25/03/1915
War Diary	Dickebush	26/03/1915	26/03/1915
War Diary	Vormezeele	27/03/1915	28/03/1915
War Diary	Dickebush	29/03/1915	30/03/1915
War Diary	Voormezeele	31/03/1915	31/03/1915
Heading	7 Inf. Bde. 3rd Div. War Diary 1st Battalion The Wiltshire Regiment April 1915		
War Diary	Voormezeele	01/04/1915	03/04/1915
War Diary	Dickebush	04/04/1915	07/04/1915
War Diary	Elzenwalle	08/04/1915	11/04/1915
War Diary	Dickebush	12/04/1915	15/04/1915
War Diary	Elzenwalle	16/04/1915	19/04/1915
War Diary	Dickebush	20/04/1915	23/04/1915
War Diary	Elzenwalle	24/04/1915	27/04/1915
War Diary	Dickebush	28/04/1915	30/04/1915
Heading	7th Inf Bde. 3rd Div. War Diary 1st Battn. The Wiltshire Regiment May 1915		
War Diary	Dickebush	01/05/1915	01/05/1915
War Diary	Elzenwalle	02/05/1915	11/05/1915
War Diary	Dickebush	12/05/1915	16/05/1915

War Diary	Elzenwalle	17/05/1915	21/05/1915
War Diary	Dickebush	22/05/1915	24/05/1915
War Diary	Elzenwalle	25/05/1915	29/05/1915
War Diary	Dickebush	30/05/1915	31/05/1915
Heading	7th Inf. Bde. 3rd Div. War Diary 1st Battn. The Wiltshire Regiment June 1915		
War Diary	Dickebush	01/06/1915	02/06/1915
War Diary	Vlamertinghe	03/06/1915	03/06/1915
War Diary	Hooge	04/06/1915	08/06/1915
War Diary	Ypres	09/06/1915	30/06/1915
Heading	7th Inf. Bde. 3rd Div. War Diary 1st Battn. The Wiltshire Regiment July 1915		
War Diary	Hooge	01/07/1915	01/07/1915
War Diary	Busseboom	02/07/1915	04/07/1915
War Diary	Hooge	05/07/1915	08/07/1915
War Diary	Busseboome	09/07/1915	11/07/1915
War Diary	Abeele	12/07/1915	20/07/1915
War Diary	St. Eloi	21/07/1915	24/07/1915
War Diary	Dickebusch Huts	25/07/1915	27/07/1915
War Diary	St. Eloi	28/07/1915	31/07/1915
Heading	7th Inf. Bde. 3rd Div. War Diary 1st Battn. The Wiltshire Regiment August 1915		
War Diary	St. Eloi	01/08/1915	02/08/1915
War Diary	St. Jean	03/08/1915	11/08/1915
War Diary	Canal Bank	12/08/1915	14/08/1915
War Diary	La Brique	15/08/1915	19/08/1915
War Diary	Ouderdon	20/08/1915	24/08/1915
War Diary	Hooge	25/08/1915	27/08/1915
War Diary	1 N.W. Dickebusche	28/08/1915	30/08/1915
War Diary	Hooge	31/08/1915	31/08/1915
Heading	7th Inf. Bde. 3rd Div. War Diary 1st Battn. The Wiltshire Regiment September 1915		
War Diary	Hooge	01/09/1915	03/09/1915
War Diary	Ypres	04/09/1915	09/09/1915
War Diary	Hooge	10/09/1915	12/09/1915
War Diary	Busseboom	13/09/1915	18/09/1915
War Diary	Ypres	19/09/1915	24/09/1915
War Diary	Hooge	24/09/1915	26/09/1915
War Diary	Bivouaces Busseboom	27/09/1915	30/09/1915
Heading	7th Inf. Bde. 3rd Div. Battn. transferred with Bde. to 25th Div. 18.10.15. War Diary 1st Battn. The Wiltshire Regiment. October 1915		
War Diary	Zillebeke	01/10/1915	16/10/1915
War Diary	Abeele	16/10/1915	17/10/1915
War Diary	Bailleul	18/10/1915	23/10/1915
War Diary	Papot	24/10/1915	31/10/1915

WO 95/1415

3 DIV 7 INFANTRY BDE

1 Battn Wiltshire Regt
August 1914 – Oct 1915

3RD DIVISION
7TH INFY BDE

1ST BATTALION
THE WILTSHIRE REGIMENT
AUG - DEC 1914

7th Brigade.
3rd Division.

1st BATTALION

THE WILTSHIRE REGIMENT

AUGUST 1 9 1 4

WAR. DIARY. 12/868

1st Batt. Wiltshire Regt.

7th Brigade

Volume I 4 — 31. 8. /14.

Attached:
Appx. I and II

WAR DIARY
or
INTELLIGENCE SUMMARY.
(Erase heading not required.)

Army Form C. 2118.

Instructions regarding War Diaries and Intelligence Summaries are contained in F.S. Regs., Part II. and the Staff Manual respectively. Title pages will be prepared in manuscript.

Hour, Date, Place	Summary of Events and Information	Remarks and references to Appendices
5.45 pm. 4-8-14. Tidworth	Order to Mobilize received. Mobilization commenced.	P.T.
6.5 am. 5-8-14	Wire stating war had broken out with Germany. First day of Mobilization. Precautionary Period detachment reported.	P.T.
6-8-14	2nd day of Mobn. Progress normal.	P.T.
7-8-14	3rd day of Mobn. Progress normal.	P.T.
8-8-14	4th day of Mobn. Mobilization completed at 6.30 pm with exception of Officers to complete establishment, which today was reduced by 1 Capt. + 2 Subs.	P.T.
9-8-14	Church parade. Route marching. Inoculation for entire. Inspections.	P.T.
10-8-14	Musketry drills and Range practice.	P.T.
11-8-14	Brigade Route March, and Range Practice. Inoculation continued.	P.T.
10.30 am. 12-8-14	Orders to entrain received.	P.T.
12-8-14	Packing up and closing accounts.	P.T.
7.22 am. 13-8-14	1st Train. Lt Col A.W. Hartell Commanding strength 505 all ranks left Tidworth.	P.T.
8.56 am. 13-8-14	2nd Train. Major A.A.S. Barnes Cmdg strength 509 all ranks left Tidworth.	P.T.
9.12 am. 13-8-14.	1st train arrived Southampton docks & detrained at Shed 23.	P.T.

Army Form C. 2118.

WAR DIARY
or
INTELLIGENCE SUMMARY.
(Erase heading not required.)

Instructions regarding War Diaries and Intelligence Summaries are contained in F. S. Regs., Part II. and the Staff Manual respectively. Title pages will be prepared in manuscript.

Hour, Date, Place	Summary of Events and Information	Remarks and references to Appendices
11 am. 13-8-14.	1st Train commenced entraining on "SS SOUTH WESTERN". Much delay in embarkation of vehicles on hatch very small and all crafts and the wheels of the G.S. wagons even had to be removed. All horses (there had to be towed and slung) and vehicles on board by 4.15 pm.	PAT.
4.15 pm "	Troops embarked.	PAT.
4.30 pm "	Vessel sailed.	PAT.
7.15 pm "	Anchored in SANDOWN BAY.	PAT.
5. am. 14-8-14.	Got under way.	PAT.
10.45 am 13-8-14.	2nd Train arrived at SOUTHAMPTON and commenced entrainRation on "SS PRINCESS ENA".	PAT.
2.30 pm "	Cast off.	
7.30 am 14-8-14.	2nd Party arrived at ROUEN and marched to camp.	PAT.
8.45 pm "	at MONT ST. AIGNAN. 1st Party arrived at ROUEN, disembarked and marched to Camp at MONT ST AIGNAN	PAT. Two men sent to civil Hospital sick on 15th inst PAT.
1.30 am. 16-8-14.	The Battalion marched from ST. AIGNAN Camp + entrained at 3.5 am at the GARE DE NORD, ROUEN.	PAT.
7.25 pm. 16-8-14.	Batt detrained at AULNOYE station and went into Billets near AULNOYE village	PAT.

Army Form C. 2118.

WAR DIARY
or
INTELLIGENCE SUMMARY.
(Erase heading not required.)

Instructions regarding War Diaries and Intelligence Summaries are contained in F. S. Regs., Part II. and the Staff Manual respectively. Title pages will be prepared in manuscript.

Hour, Date, Place	Summary of Events and Information	Remarks and references to Appendices
7 am. 17-8-14.	Battalion marched in Brigade via LEVAL to MARBAIX. and went into Billets	PRC
18-8-14.	Rested in Billets. Battalion route march.	PRC
19-8-14.	Remained in Billets. Battalion Route march. Took over the protective posts round MARBAIX.	PRC
20-8-14.	Battalion in Billets. Brigade Route march to AVESNES. Great Reception by inhabitants; Troops decked with flowers.	PRC
21-8-14.	Marched at 4.40 from Billets via DOMPIERRE and MAUBERGE to FEIGNIES arrived at 12.30 billeted for the night.	PRC
22-8-14.	Marched at 7am from Billets via GOGNIES - BOUGNIES and ASQUILLE to CIPLY went into Billets."C" Company on Outpost to HARMIGNIES. GERMAN aeroplane passed over.	PRC
15:10. 22-8-14.	Orders to send one Company to NOUVELLES to protect artillery. C. Company detailed. This company afterwards moved to HARMIGNIES.	PRC
4 P.M. 23-8-14.	Three companies ordered to entrench position on N. of CIPLY facing MONS, where shelled by enemy whilst doing so and until nightfall. Entrenching continued throughout night.	HWPM

WAR DIARY
or
INTELLIGENCE SUMMARY.
(Erase heading not required.)

Army Form C. 2118.

Hour, Date, Place	Summary of Events and Information	Remarks and references to Appendices
23 24th—8-14	Battle of MONS, regiment did not take part in the engagement, beyond entrenching at CIPLY.	Source—
24—8-14.	Battle of CIPLY— Enemy started about dawn to shell with trenches and continued bombardment throughout day, till about 1 P.M. when 7th Inf Bde was ordered to retire to St WAAST. Casualties in trenches Captain Knowes and 3 men killed Captain and Adjutant Rowan wounded and about 20 men. C.O's horse shot under him — Retirement to St WAAST effected without further loss enemy following up leisurely.	HUTCH.
25-8-14	7th Inf Bde retired to position # at GOMMIGNIES and were driven out by enemy's superior forces returning on SOLESMES, where at dusk WILTS and South Lancs fought a rearguard action.	HUTCH.

Army Form C. 2118.

WAR DIARY
or
INTELLIGENCE SUMMARY.
(Erase heading not required.)

Instructions regarding War Diaries and Intelligence Summaries are contained in F. S. Regs., Part II. and the Staff Manual respectively. Title pages will be prepared in manuscript.

Hour, Date, Place	Summary of Events and Information	Remarks and references to Appendices
25-8-14	and after some engagement retired under cover of darkness to COURY, enemy did not pursue but shelled the town of SOLESMES.	HWCu
26-8-14	Battle of COURY — LE CATEAU. WILTS held E. NE of COURY the whole morning were heavily shelled and attacked by infantry and suffered 80 to 100 casualties. The following officers were wounded Lieut Loder-Symonds, Brown and Carrington — when retirement was ordered WILTS fell back to BEAUREVOIR.	HWCu
27-8-14	At 2 a.m retired to HAGICOURT where halted a few hours and then retired to VERMAND, halted for four hours and then continued retirement to HAM. WILTS found advanced guard during night march	HWCu

WAR DIARY
or
INTELLIGENCE SUMMARY.
(Erase heading not required.)

Army Form C. 2118.

Hour, Date, Place	Summary of Events and Information	Remarks and references to Appendices
28-8-14	3rd Division continued retirement to NOYON and billeted at village of TARLEFERE.	HWON
29-8-14	About 1 p.m. WILTS and remainder of 7 Inf Bde moved into woods to North to prevent enemy's outflanking movement and occupied outpost position during the night.	HWOE
30-8-14	About 4 a.m. 7 Inf Bde fell back from village of SALENCY across the river OISE to near VARENNES. Being the last Bde to cross the river, bridges over the river were blown up. Fell back to Vic. Sur AISNE where WILTS found outposts to the Bde for the night 30 Aug/31 Aug.	HWTW HWTW
31-8-14.	About 8.15 a.m. withdrew from outpost position exchange of shots between B Coy and Uhlan Patrol	HWTW

App. I.

Army Form B. 231.

Unit. ~~[redacted]~~
Place.
Date 19.8.1914

FIELD STATE.

To be rendered in accordance with Field Service Regulations, Part II.

Unit	FIGHTING STRENGTH (This should *not* include attached details, 2nd line transport, details who march with 2nd line transport, or any men unfit to fight.)						RATION STRENGTH (To include fighting strength, attached details, 2nd line transport and all personnel and animals attached for rations and forage.)		
	Personnel		Horses and Mules		Guns and ammunition wagons (stating nature)	Machine guns	Remarks	Personnel	Horses and Mules	
	Officers	Other Ranks	Riding	Draught and pack				Total all ranks entitled to rations	Heavy horses with R.G.A.	Other horses and mules
1st Bn. Wiltshire Regt. R.A.M.C.	25 1	968	13 +5	+1 +9	S.A.A. carts 6	2		1020	—	62
Totals ...	26	969	13	+1	6	2		1020	—	62

Ammunition with unit:—
 ·303-inch; approximate number of rounds per man 220
 ·303-inch;   ”   ”   ”   , machine gun 11500
 Gun or howitzer; approximate number of rounds per gun or howitzer _____

Supplies with unit:—
 Approximate number of days' rations for men of ration strength One
      ”   ”   ”   , forage for animals   ”   One

(Signature of Commander)

Copy. Off. 1 (A)

LANDING RETURN.

No. of Report
(For use in 3rd Echelon, General Headquarters.)

To be furnished by all Arms, Services and Departments to the Military Landing Officer at the place of landing for despatch to the 3rd Echelon, General Headquarters.

Place __Rouen.__ Date __14-8-14.__

Return showing numbers rationed by, and Transport on charge of *__1st Tramload 1st Batt. Wiltshire Regiment__

Detail.	Personnel.								Animals.			Guns, carriages and limbers, and transport vehicles.											Remarks.
	Officers.	Warrant officers.	Serjeants.	Trumpeters, &c.	Corporals.	Bombardiers and 2nd corporals.	Privates, gunners and sappers / Troopers or drivers.	Total all ranks.	Horses. Riding.	Horses. Draught.	Horses. Pack.	Mules.	Guns, carriages and limbers, showing description.	Ammunition wagons and limbers.	Machine guns.	Horsed. 4-wheeled.	Horsed. 2-wheeled.	Motor cars.	Tractors.	Lorries. Mechanical. Workshop trucks. Water tanks. Travelling vans. Trailers.	Motor bicycles.	Bicycles.	
Effective strength of unit or training. ~~Blood question~~	13	1	27	-	21	-	436 / 3	501	8	17	4	-	-	-	-	4	5	-	-	- - - - -	-	9	
	1		1				3								1							4	4 Driver Cycle Coy
+Casualties during journey.																							
Total casualties ...																							
Landing strength ...	13	1	28	-	21	-	439 / 3	505	8	17	4	-	-	-	-	4	5	-	-	- - - - -	-	13	
Wanting to complete.																							

* Insert name of unit, stating if complete or a trainload of the same. † Details of casualties are to be shown on the back of this form.

Sgd O Hasted. Lt.Col. Signature of Commander.
Cmdg 1st Wilts Regt.

(670) N.B.—This return will be rendered in place of those mentioned in paragraph 1652, King's Regulations.

7th Brigade.
3rd Division.

1st BATTALION

THE WILTSHIRE REGIMENT

SEPTEMBER 1 9 1 4::

No 1

1st Wiltshire Regt. 121/1230

7th Brigade

Vol II.

(with Appendices to Vol I.
[Extended to planning with Vol I] 30.9.14

Attached :—
Apps. III & VII.

Army Form C. 2118.

(Signed)

WAR DIARY
or
INTELLIGENCE SUMMARY.
(Erase heading not required.)

Instructions regarding War Diaries and Intelligence Summaries are contained in F. S. Regs., Part II. and the Staff Manual respectively. Title pages will be prepared in manuscript.

Hour, Date, Place	Summary of Events and Information	Remarks and references to Appendices

D. A. G.
3rd Echelon
Base.

Herewith originals of War Diary
1st Wiltshire Regt. for the month
of September. Also appendices for
August & September, the former was
omitted last month.

2-10-14.   Major
  Cmdg. 1st Wilts Regt.

[Note: Appendices for August 1914
have been extracted and
place with August 1914 diary
all
]

31-8-14	Relvd by C...
	hot and t...
1-9-14	At 7.30 a.m
	7th Inf Bde lin...
	a Bde of the 8...
	to VILLERS S...
2-9-14	At 2 a.m W...
	retirement...
	rearguard t...
	for the day...
	Outpost P...
	On BARCY...
	3rd Worcest Regt.

WAR DIARY
or
INTELLIGENCE SUMMARY.
(Erase heading not required.)

Army Form C. 2118.

Hour, Date, Place	Summary of Events and Information	Remarks and references to Appendices
31-8-14	Relieved to COYOLLES, WILTS rearguard to Bde, very hot and trying march	HUTCH
1-9-14	At 7.30 am retired towards LÉVIGNEN where the 7th Inf Bde turned back to cover the retirement of a Bde of the 5th Division, withdrawing about 5 pm to VILLERS St GENEST where we remained the night.	HUTCH
2-9-14	At 2 am WILTS took up a position to cover the retirement of remainder of Bde, withdrawing as rearguard to MARCILLY where rearguard halted for the day, at dusk WILTS took up an outpost position for the night with our right on BARCY, our left being prolonged by the 3rd Worcester regt.	HUTCH

WAR DIARY
or
INTELLIGENCE SUMMARY.

Army Form C. 2118.

Hour, Date, Place	Summary of Events and Information	Remarks and references to Appendices
3-9-14	Withdrew from outpost position at 4.45 a.m. relied on PRINGY, where we were ordered to find a right flank guard at BARCY for the 3rd Division returning on MEAUX. Reached Meaux about 12 noon crossed river MARNE one coy detailed field left bank of river until blowing up of bridge completed. Retired and bivouaced at SANCY arriving at 6 p.m.	HWCH
4-9-14	Stalled at SANCY until 11 p.m. when WILTS marched to CHATRÉS. Billeting at a farm with 74th Bde H.Qrs about 1 mile N. of CHATRES.	
5-9-14	First reinforcement consisting of Captain Reynolds 3rd Bn and 89 rank and file joined the battalion 8-2 N.C.O's and men of this reinforcement being posted to A coy.	HWCH

WAR DIARY or INTELLIGENCE SUMMARY

Army Form C. 2118.

Hour, Date, Place	Summary of Events and Information	Remarks and references to Appendices
6-9-14 (Sunday)	The Advance N commenced. Batt. marched as Advance Guard of the Brigade at head of the Division. Advanced thro Forest of Crecy. Halted for some time. The turned N.E. advanced on little village of HAUTEFEVILLE which had evidently been just vacated by the enemy. Advance again. Arrived at dusk passed thro FONTETELLE where a certain amount of firing on to Advance Guard by enemy piquets took place. Crossed bridge of over R. MORIN which was however only lightly held by enemy. Pushed on up to high ground near the village of LE CHARNOIS about 2 kilos N of FAREMOUTIERS arriving there about 1 am. Took up an outpost line there. Both moved up on our right.	
7-9-14 (Monday)	Didn't arrive till dawn. Slightly attacked. Both our right suffering some casualties. At 2 pm 5th Division to take up an line he retired to FAREMOUTIERS & billeted for 2½ hours marched at 6 pm thro COULOMMIERS where we picked up second reinforcement of about 90 men under Lt Watson. Billeted at paper mill about 2 kilos E of COULOMMIERS	

WAR DIARY or INTELLIGENCE SUMMARY.

(Erase heading not required.)

Army Form C. 2118.

Hour, Date, Place	Summary of Events and Information	Remarks and references to Appendices
8 Sept 1914 (Tuesday)	Marched 7 am. thro REBAIS about where we halted some time while 8th Brigade were engaged about ORLY. From there taking our division at about dusk. We pushed on to village of BOISSIRES where we bivouacked. Nothing for night.	
9 Sept 1914 (Wednesday)	Advanced N through NANTEUIL where we crossed the R. MARNE. Passing hot opened bridge intact. Passed thro CROUTTES and just N of here we were delayed most of day thro enemy having command N of the road with his guns. There a detachment through the woods and reached BEZU LE GUERY at dusk here we found up with 5th Division. Billets being kept at dusk at MONTREUIL. 2 miles N.W.	
10 Sept 1914 (Thursday)	Advanced thro VEVILLY - CHEZY. To position W of DAMMARD where WILTSHIRE & S. LANCS. Regt found outposts. The bivouac. Captured about 5 to 600 foreseeing the day.	
11 Sept 1914 (Friday)	Advanced N.E. thro DAMMARD to GRAND ROZOY day turned but and cold. Very little room to billets has got very wet, and spent an uncomfortable night.	

WAR DIARY or INTELLIGENCE SUMMARY

(Erase heading not required.)

Army Form C. 2118.

Hour, Date, Place	Summary of Events and Information	Remarks and references to Appendices
12 Sept 1914. Sat	Marched 9.20 being 3rd Regt to move. A showery day gradually turning very hot, a lot of delay on the Road. Advanced Guard got to BRAINE 2nd Bde as far as CERSEUIL when we bivouacked into any cover from the rain. We were wet.	
13 Sept 1914 (Sunday)	Advance 7-20 am from through BRAINE. Known during by shell fire a road between BRAINE & CHASSEMY. Battn billeted for day in entrenched gunbn off the road about N of BRAINE. Bivouacked in field near BRAINE for night. Delay due to enemy having blown up all bridges over to RAISNE.	
14 Sept 1914 (Monday)	Marched at 5 am as Adv Guard to Brigade through BRENELLE. The left flanned E of CHASSEMY. Pushed on from here to cross the R AISNE at VAILLY when bridge had been by Engineer during the night. Were under fire from enemy's artillery. While here 8th & 9th Bdes who had crossed the river under cover of ourselves advanced on ridges in N. bank of R G.O.C. 8th Bde asked for 1 Batt. WR sent to his assistance Wiltshire Regt sent off and took up position by the bridge & own by railway bridge between VAILLY & PRESLES. This bridge was demolished but a plank had been put down to leach.	

Army Form C. 2118.

WAR DIARY
or
INTELLIGENCE SUMMARY.
(Erase heading not required.)

Instructions regarding War Diaries and Intelligence Summaries are contained in F. S. Regs., Part II. and the Staff Manual respectively. Title pages will be prepared in manuscript.

Hour, Date, Place	Summary of Events and Information	Remarks and references to Appendices
14th Sept 1914 (Monday)	On approaching the bridge the Battn. on the right of the 9th Brigade who were on the right of our position across the AISNE were seen to be falling back and had already reached the Pontoon Railway Bridge. Bttn. at once took up a position to cover their retirement. 2nd R. Irish Reg. 2 R.I.R. had arrived to assume command the position of the Brigade. Colonel Bird issued an advance to seize the hill to the N. part of which was still held by the 9th Brigade. The Battn. crossed by the broken bridge just on the hill N.E. of ST PREARD N[?] VAILLY the Coy being on the right A Coy having some casualties in getting thro'. The R. Irish Rifles then crossed and prolonged the line to our left (to West). Battn. took up an outpost line at dusk and entrenched. The enemy made a half hearted attack about 11 pm. which was not followed our position having shelled had several casualties. Ammunition came up in support. A last night. Enemy again made another half hearted attack which was supported by their artillery about 11 pm.	
15 Sept 1914 (Tuesday)		

WAR DIARY
or
INTELLIGENCE SUMMARY.
(Erase heading not required.)

Army Form C. 2118.

Hour, Date, Place	Summary of Events and Information	Remarks and references to Appendices
16 Sept 1914 (Wednesday)	Still in same position. 2nd Cavalry Brigade came up in our right and this linked us up with L Division of the 2nd Division in the East. Enemy been entrenching a position 2000 yards to our N.E. in front of position held by Lt Inf Bde. Guards on our right pushed forward a patrol at night + drove the enemy from line about TOLEM PRISE farm.	
17th Sept 1914 (Thursday)	Remained in same position. Rained all day. Some R.E. came up after dark to assist Engineers in our entrenchments. An attack by night thought probable. It didn't come off. A very cold night.	
18 Sept 1914 (Friday)	Remained in same position. Was shelled every day, and had small trouble with patrols. A wet night.	
19th Sept 1914 (Saturday)	No change in disposition. Very heavily shelled in afternoon. Enemy pushed forward an attack about 5-30 pm which was repulsed.	

Army Form C. 2118.

WAR DIARY
or
INTELLIGENCE SUMMARY.
(Erase heading not required.)

Instructions regarding War Diaries and Intelligence Summaries are contained in F.S. Regs., Part II. and the Staff Manual respectively. Title pages will be prepared in manuscript.

Hour, Date, Place	Summary of Events and Information	Remarks and references to Appendices
27th Septr 1914 (Sunday)	3 reinforcements of about 90 rank & file under 2 Lt Blackett arrived & took up positions of companies. Enemy in groups from 1 to about 10 men between 8 + 9 am attacked in about 11 to 12 hours a party of enemy estimated at 200 & 2 machine guns got through some dense bush on to line & rushing on got on flanks of the rear of trenches held by Worcestershire Regt and thus took to line of the front. Enemy pushed on and seriously threatened to right of our position, but eventually stopped within 50 to 100 yards of our position (as it then was). During this time a lot of close fighting took place. One of our guns on our right was shelled knocked hilly & enemy with very good effect. Enemy fell back a little & started intrenching themselves in two commanding & almost bare knolls which they had gained. Our fire again drove him out of these. While all this was happening C, B + D Coys from West to East on a high ground above held the position. But were engaged with parties of the enemy sent to try & work round their rear. At 5 pm a general advance ordered with all troops on right. (About 200 men of Wiltshire, Worcester & Gloucester Regts)	For account of the enemy report sent in to Bde in 2 & 3' left a duplicate of which is in Correspondence book. [signed] app. III

WAR DIARY or INTELLIGENCE SUMMARY.

Army Form C. 2118.

Hour, Date, Place	Summary of Events and Information	Remarks and references to Appendices
20th Sept. (Continued)	At 5.45 pm we regained our former line connected with the Coldstreams on our left. Enemy retired having many dead & wounded. In the fight the Batt. had Lt. Col. Arnold Coney wounded, Capt Reynolds, Lt Cruickshank killed, & Lts Rosewarne & Lloyd wounded and about 80 Rank & file killed wounded or missing. Major T. Robb was ordered to take command of the Battalion when 1st Right Section of the were led by the 2nd Bn of Bks, in which were also 1 Coy Worcestershire Regt, 1 Coy S Lancashire Regt. This section was reinforced on the right by 4 Machine Guns 2of the 12 Lancers & 2 of the 16th Hussars. No further attack that night. Informed that Brigade would be relieved by another later that night	2nd Lt Rosewarne died of his wounds some time 25
21st Sept. 1914 (Monday)	Endeavoured to make position more tenable difficult of entry. Skilled Battn. got 2 new Machine Guns & were there about 6 pm. 4 "Black" on our right attacked about 6 pm. An attempt to draw our fire by the enemy firing at long range from his trenches was made at 9 pm and was seriously from enemy point of view as almost continual fusillade held up throughout the night in rear part of the line. This held firing at night badly hurt & checking & discouraging	

WAR DIARY
or
INTELLIGENCE SUMMARY.
(Erase heading not required.)

Army Form C. 2118.

Instructions regarding War Diaries and Intelligence Summaries are contained in F. S. Regs., Part II. and the Staff Manual respectively. Title pages will be prepared in manuscript.

Hour, Date, Place	Summary of Events and Information	Remarks and references to Appendices
22 Sept 14 (Tuesday)	Shropshire LI, 16th Rds (less R Coys) Brown arrived at 4 am & took over front of Right Section relieving C & R Coys before daylight. Northants Regt Remainder of 7th Bn Bde & HQ withdrew during early morning to BRAINE & bivouacked. Wiltshire Regt & Coy S Lancaster Regt ordered to stand fast in their position till relieved following night by Norfolk Regt. Movement across the pontoon bridge at VAILLY being only possible at night. he has been temporarily under Command of G.O.C. 16th Infantry Brigade. Norfolks arrived at 9 pm & took over Wiltshire Section of line. Heavy rifle firing took place just as they were relieving. Wiltshires & S Lancs Coy arrived Bethen at 10 pm & bivouaced off for VAILLY where he picked up on fire & transport moved to AISNE & reached BRAINE at 12.30 am on 23 Sept where he went into billets having been 9 days on the position N of the River, where the hardships were considerable.	
23 Sept 1914 Wednesday	In billets at BRAINE. Battn visited by General Sir Horace Smith-Dorrien K.C.B. Commanding 2nd Corps & also by General H. Hamilton Commdg III Division G.O.C. II Corps made an address to as many men as could be got together at the square of the Market, and spoke in very flattering terms of the conduct of the Battn.	

WAR DIARY
or
INTELLIGENCE SUMMARY.

Army Form C. 2118.

Hour, Date, Place	Summary of Events and Information	Remarks and references to Appendices
23 Sept 1914. (Continued)	4th Reinforcement of about 10 who were 2nd Lieuts arrived & posted. Estimated that Battn. lost in Killed wounded missing during the occupation of N bank right bank of the R AISNE about 460 all ranks. Estimated casualties since arrival in country with the following " " up to date. Officers Killed — Wounded — Missing — Total Officers 3 — 9 — nil — 12 Other ranks Killed — Wounded — Missing — Total ranks 37 — 200 — 125 — 362 Strength on arrival in country 1000 approx. 4 reinforcements (about 90 each) 360 " 1360 Deduct 360 Killed wounded missing Balance 1000. I find present strength of Battn. is as follows. with Coys 800 men A.D.S. etc 125. The difference of about 95 rank file is that 22 Officers + 925 men made up by Men sick returns who have dropped out	

WAR DIARY
or
INTELLIGENCE SUMMARY.
(Erase heading not required.)

Army Form C. 2118.

Hour, Date, Place	Summary of Events and Information	Remarks and references to Appendices
24th Sept. 1914 (Thursday)	Battn in Billets at BRAINE refitting, reorganizing & resting for the first time since 21st of August. Major Panter received an order to report himself at the Base & was during up 31st August sent to D.A.C. 3' Echelon Base. Captain & Adjutant P.S. Rowan who was wounded at CIPLY on 23 August 16 reported for duty and resumed his duties as Adjutant. Checked strength, Battalion stood 22 offrs 922 other Ranks. Received orders to proceed to BRENELLE to entrench position. Marched at 1.20 p.m. entrenched line from BRENELLE village due EAST to 300× WEST of point 175. Had few tools other than light entrenching tools. Returned to BRAINE at 7 p.m. Trenches almost completed. Recommendations for professionals needed.	Field State ⊞ App. IV
25th Sept. 1914 (Friday)	Rested in Billets refitting and overhauling. Death reported on 7th F. Ambulance of 2nd Lt. Ponsonwere who was wounded NORTH of the AISNE on Sept. 20th	⊟ App. V ⊞ Field State rendered App. VI
26th Sept. 1914 (Saturday) 4.20 am. 27th Sept. 1914. Saturday	Received orders to proceed to CHASSEMY to reinforce 2nd R.I.R. as Germans were reported to have crossed CONDÉ bridge. Reached wood of ANCIENNE, BRAINE - CHASSÉMY road, where Bn halted & sent out patrols. Report re Germans proved false. Bn returned to	

Army Form C. 2118.

WAR DIARY
or
INTELLIGENCE SUMMARY.
(Erase heading not required.)

Instructions regarding War Diaries and Intelligence Summaries are contained in F.S. Regs., Part II. and the Staff Manual respectively. Title pages will be prepared in manuscript.

Hour, Date, Place	Summary of Events and Information	Remarks and references to Appendices
10.15 am. 27th Sept.	BRAINE at 8.10 am.	W.
	B + C. Coy. marched out to entrench position on BRAINE - DHUIZEL road; returned at 3 pm, on relief by A + D Coys who returned at 7 pm.	W.
2.20 am. 28th Sept. 1914 (Monday)	Orders to turn out and proceed to CHASSEMY. Bn left at 2.50 am and reached road 1½ miles S. of CHASSEMY at 4 am. Reported to O.C. CHASSEMY and found our posts. Remained halted till 5.55 am when Bn returned to BRAINE	W.
11.10 am. 28th Sept.	Received orders to proceed to CHASSEMY and relieve 2nd R.I.R. by 5 pm.	W.
2.30 pm. 28th Sept.	marched to CHASSEMY by covered route and took over outpost line from the 2nd R.I.R. 'A' Coy in Reserve, remainder and M.G. Section in outpost line. 1st + 6th Divisions in the trenches were engaged but our outpost remained. CHASSEMY was shelled for a time no casualties.	For orders of outpost portion see App. VII
29th Sept. 1914. (Tuesday)	Stood to arms at 4.30 am. No change in the outpost line.	W.
30th Sept. 1914 (Wednesday)	Stood to arms at 4.30 am. No change in the outpost line.	W.

App. III ~~BC~~ 4

Report on attack on the Right sector
of the 7th Infantry Brigade on Sunday 3 September

Between 7 am & the date to Border
R.D.F. a sudden heavy [fire?] was made and
also reinforced by rifle fire. left the attack had been
foreseen. My platoon No 4 [of?] [?] sports
[?] and [?] masked in [?] of the [?]
Commanding the centre of the lines of L.T. Harris
reported [?] [?] [?] [?] M.R.E
across the point. his brother died [?] the
place in [?] an [?] [?] [?] [?]
[?] then facing the place was [?]
and held by the [?] [?] [?]
[?] on a [?] of [?] [?]
[?] [?] [?] [?] [?] [?]
the [?] [?] platoon moving to attack
advanced [?] [?] [?] [?] [?]
[?] [?] [?] [?] [?] to the [?]
opened [?] [?] [?] [?] [?] [?]
that [?] [?] [?] N.W. were [?]

5

and unobserved got through some thick wood —
where there was no track almost to the N of the Wiltshire
Regt H.Q. shown on map. Having massed from 150 to
200 men here they rushed down on to a little hill on the left
of the WORCESTER trenches (hill marked R on sketch)
from here they enfiladed the WORCESTER trenches
and were in fact almost behind them.

From here they inflicted much loss on the WORCESTERS
and meanwhile pushed forward in the line of
their original advance direct against the
WORCESTER trenches. bringing up 2 Machine
guns along the ride through the wood opposite
the W in WORCESTERSHIRE on the sketch.

A heavy flanking fire was now poured into the
the S corner of the wood by my Company from
about Point X. Which for a time delayed
them. but the party of Germans who had got
onto hill R pressed down getting the WORCESTER
trenches and bringing a fire on my Company

6

at about point X and some of the WORCESTER who were also there. While these men were going on the transport about point X were subjected to heavy fire from the German artillery, both high explosive — shrapnel being used against us.

The Germans have a lamp post in the fields about point S. Near the corner of the wood. Commenced trying on the ruses described in appendix A. I was at point X myself and can corroborate what Tudor said in his statement. I was told by him I saw them fire on two, three occasions on account of our men coming up with the enemy, and were afraid of hitting them. I did not see that the West Germans have without their rifles + equipment. While this parleying whatever the surrender was in progress. Meanwhile the Germans have been passing on behind this line of (Germans) who talked surrender

7

The Germans eventually got a maxim gun & track
commanding track about point S. and fired down along
it. As far as I am aware I used my men at to go
up to accept these Germans surrender, but I am
sure they got a few men by that time.

N. Regt were now reinforced by some of the S. LANCS
Regt. some of whom held the S edge of the wood by
point marked Z. The Germans penetrated up to within
a short distance of them but I believe came beyond
this portion of wood. While we retired from here
to the road leading from point X down to what
Bde H.Q.

After a short time a gun of ? vis / mm about
15 cwt 2000 yds to the S.E. shelled this portion
of wood by point Z. and apparently caused
the Germans to retire towards the little knolls
marked R & P. There they brought a machine
gun into action & started entrenching

8

This movement on the part of the German guns was seen from these trees. But being seen by the guns before mentioned some well placed rounds of shrapnel caused considerable loss. This being consistent temporarily abandon their shielding guns. He started to bring along his limbers, but one was knocked from its tree close [illegible]. At about this juncture I received a report that Col Hazard was wounded — He requested to take command of the Battery. I remained where I was on the Ridge.

Sometime about 3 p.m. he [asked?] the [Brigadier?] [illegible] for [me?] to [ride?] his [Battn?] and advised he [?] make a move forward in a N direction to [take?] the ridge [?] the [?]. And [formed?] on our [original?] position and [?] up [with?] the remaining 2 [Coys?] of my Regt (B & D) [?] now [?] their [original?] position at [?] ground.

9

The moment we started to move forward we were again
heavily shelled about point X.

Before I moved forward about 1 Coy S. Staffordshire Regt
arrived at about point X to support us. Their
approach being seen was I think the cause for this
shelling.

○ We advanced through the woods without any further
opposition + regained the required line and
connection with the other companies of the Wiltshire
Regt. by about 5.45 pm.

Steps were then taken to complete the line + fell
any possible avenues of approach & put sentries
to watch out posts.

○ On our way up about the knolls K & P. also about
the track near point S. we found several dead +
wounded Germans, rifles + ammunition etc.

I afterwards went along the line held by my
Regt. and found that the Germans had detached
a party to work W from the knoll K. This

10

engaged B. Corps from the rear - this prevented the
from having their penetration - put spurs to ?
cut off Germans off.

I cannot say in what numbers the Germans were
but I am led to suppose the people put they
been believe to have had about a Regt (? Battn)
there, anyhow apparently one pushed back a
force of this size and must I think have kept
a large number behind them ? he took 150
had 2 Battn there

the above account is what I gleaned from
what I saw of the fight from what passed
& purely ad hoc time.

A good deal of close fighting appears to have
taken place about the H Bthre Regt H.Q. —
post (?) (?) truth to judging by the positions
of the Confederate killed & wounded after
the engagement   /Aleck Major
22 Sept 14.   1st Matthew Regt

Rough sketch of position on Sunday 20 Sept 1914.

TO OSTEL

Track to TOLEMPRIE FARM
GERMAN POSITION

LINE OF GERMAN ADVANCE

Thick & dense WOOD

A
D
D Coy
B
C Coy
B Coy

Right of R. Irish Rifles
Left hits in R. Irish Rifles

ride
ride
Staff killed here
11000

1170 m

HQ K
Wilts Regt
Worcestershire Regt
P
Bn HQ

Open space
raked by
Enemy artillery
& MG fire

X
A Coy by day
S 1 A Coy
Z 2 p.m.

Road wet bank on N side

main road

R. AISNE

From VAILLY
½ mile

bivouac by day
TO CHAVONNE
4 R.B.

N
E
W

Rough outline of woods in brown.

GERMAN POSITION lay roughly 1000 y to the N of us.

R/9/15

MESSAGES AND SIGNALS.

Prefix	Code	Words	Received	Sent, or sent out	Office Stamp.
	£ s. d.		From	At m.	
Charges to collect			By	To	
Service Instructions:				By	

Handed in at the _____ Office, at _____ .m. Received here at _____ .m.

TO 9th T.B.

Sender's Number.	Day of Month.	In reply to Number.	AAA
5 the 2	20th September		

I enclose a rough sketch of the estimated dispositions of the enemy. There appears to me to be two alternatives.

1. The Artillery to shell the trenches and banks shown, as well as the wood marked "X" (which is were R. Brig. R.F.A shelled yesterday) to the N. and N.W.

2. To drive the wood to a point about level with X just to clear up the side, even temporarily, but this forward position could not be held and it would require at least 2 companies to carry this out.

FROM ....
PLACE ....
TIME 10 in the .... 8.10 a.m.

45

Point where Observation Officer of R.F.A. stood on the 19th inst.

new German trench

ridge with reverties with

X small trees low spur

Wood

low banks behind which men are rushing & collecting from wood on West

Plough + Roots

Northumberland Fusiliers' Trenches

Wood   Wood

NORTH

App. IV

Army Form B. 231.

Copy

FIELD STATE.

Unit 1st Bn. Wiltshire Regt.
Place ~~[redacted]~~
Date 25.9.14

To be rendered in accordance with Field Service Regulations, Part II.

Unit.	FIGHTING STRENGTH (This should *not* include attached details, 2nd line transport, details who march with 2nd line transport, or any men unfit to fight.)								RATION STRENGTH (To include fighting strength, attached details, 2nd line transport and all personnel and animals attached for rations and forage.)		
	Personnel		Horses and Mules		Guns and ammunition wagons (stating nature)	Machine guns	Remarks	Personnel	Horses and Mules		Remarks
	Officers	Other Ranks	Riding	Draught and pack				Total all ranks entitled to rations	Heavy horses with R.G.A.	Other horses and mules
1st Bn. Wiltshire Regt.	21	892	13	39	5 A A Carts 6	2		939	—	61
R A M C	1	5						34		
A S Corps										
Totals ...	22	897	13	39	6	2		9+x 3 961	—	61

Ammunition with unit:—
.303-inch; approximate number of rounds per man 220
.303-inch; " " " " machine gun 11000
Gun or howitzer; approximate number of rounds per gun or howitzer 20000

Supplies with unit:—
Approximate number of days' rations for men of ration strength one
" " " forage for animals " one

(Signature of Commander)

App V   15

1st Bn Wiltshire Regt

List of Recommendations for Good Service in the Field

No. 6591. Coy Quartermaster Sergeant WILLIAM GEORGE LESTER.

No. 7269. Sergeant ALBERT LODDER.
(Since deceased)

No. 8945. L/Cpl G.W. STREET.

The name CQMS LESTER has previously forwarded by [illegible] in connection with the action at CHIVRES. I am [illegible] it was [illegible] by you yesterday, and and to point out that [illegible] has [illegible] been [illegible] put [illegible] by [illegible].

Statement of [illegible] for distinguishing in each case are attached.

T. Nicks Major
5 Sept 14   CC 1 Wiltshire Rgt

Statement re Services of No 4591
Coy Quarter Master Sergt. W G Lester

When the retirement at CAUDRY started on the 26th August 1914, I am informed that this N.C.O. gave the greatest assistance in helping to rally men of all Corps, and keep them under control. And also in the subsequent retirement from there.

28 Sept 14

J Roche Major
OC 1st Wiltshire Regt

To O.C 1/Wiltshire Regt
25.9.14

Sir
I have the honour to submit the name of Coy Quartermaster Sergt. Lester for having done extremely good work at VAILLY from Sept 13th until Sept 23rd. During these dates Supplies had to be brought across the VAILLY BRIDGES under fire from the Enemys Guns. Coy Sgt Q.M.S Lester showed great coolness & control over his men in getting the Rations across. It was mainly due to the good work of Q.M.S Lester, that his Regt received their regular rations during the dates Sept 13th until Sept 23rd.

H Wand-Fetley Lieut
1st Wiltshire Regt
7th Bde
3rd Division

11

99

From
O.C D Coy 1/Wiltshire Regt

To Adjutant 1/Wiltshire Regt

I have the honour to forward for the favourable consideration and recommendation of the Commanding Officer the name of No 7269 Sergeant Albert Lodder in the company under my command for the Distinguished Conduct Medal. The facts of the case are as follows:- On the 20th Sept 1914 about 11.30 A.M. after the enemy had broken through a portion of our out post line, north of the river AISNE, I ordered the N.C.O to take about ten men (all that were available at the time) and endeavour to capture two of the enemy's machine guns which were causing considerable damage to our troops. This party was led with skill and courage against greatly superior numbers, and had three men wounded (of which one was the Sgt in question). The party accounted for 4 of the enemy. Owing to the paucity of the men under his command and the fact that the N.C.O. was badly wounded together with two of his comrades, as mentioned above, he was unable to successfully carry out his mission.

This N.C.O. has on several occasions during the absence of his platoon officer handled and controlled his men exceedingly well, and at all times displayed energy and zeal in his work.

I regret to say that this N.C.O. died of his wound two days after the events narrated

25/9/14

Sd. T W Stoddart Capt.
O.C. D Coy
1/Wiltshire Regt.

Statement of Reasons for Recommending

No 6105 Lance Corporal C Street
1st Wiltshire Regt.

While engaged with enemy on the right bank of the AISNE between the 16th & 22nd Sept I on two occasions sent this NCO out to the front towards TOLEMPRISE Farm. On the first occasion he and his patrol remained out all day in touch with the enemy, about whose movements & dispositions he gave me good information. He also on this occasion attempted to rescue 2 or 3 wounded men of the 9th Brigade who were lying out to the front within close range of the enemy's position, but which attempt he had to abandon owing to the enemy's fire. He did get up & bring these men back after dark. On the second occasion he held on all day in an observation post though heavily shelled. On the 20th inst after being temporarily knocked out by a blow from a stone or piece of a high explosive shell continued to command his section in the firing line

App. VI

Army Form B. 231.

FIELD STATE.

Unit. _Copy_
Place. _____
Date _26 9 14_

To be rendered in accordance with Field Service Regulations, Part II.

Unit.	FIGHTING STRENGTH (This should *not* include attached details, 2nd line transport, details who march with 2nd line transport, or any men unfit to fight.)							RATION STRENGTH (To include fighting strength, attached details, 2nd line transport and all personnel and animals attached for rations and forage.)			
	Personnel		Horses and Mules		Guns and ammunition wagons (stating nature)	Machine guns	Remarks	Personnel	Horses and Mules		Remarks
	Officers	Other Ranks	Riding	Draught and pack				Total all ranks entitled to rations	Heavy horses with R.G.A.	Other horses and mules	
1st Bn Wiltshire Regiment	20	891	13	39	S.A.A. carts 6	2		911		61	
R.A.M.C.								6			
A.S.C.								4			
3rd Bgd. of Infantry (Telephone)								2			
Totals ...	20	891	13	39	6	2		923		61	

Ammunition with unit:—
  ·303-inch; approximate number of rounds per man _326_
  ·303-inch;   „   „   „   „   machine gun _11500_
  Gun or howitzer; approximate number of rounds per gun or howitzer _✓_

Supplies with unit:—
  Approximate number of days' rations for men of ration strength _One_
         „   „   „   „   „   forage for animals _One_

J. Noel Hope
(Signature of Commander)

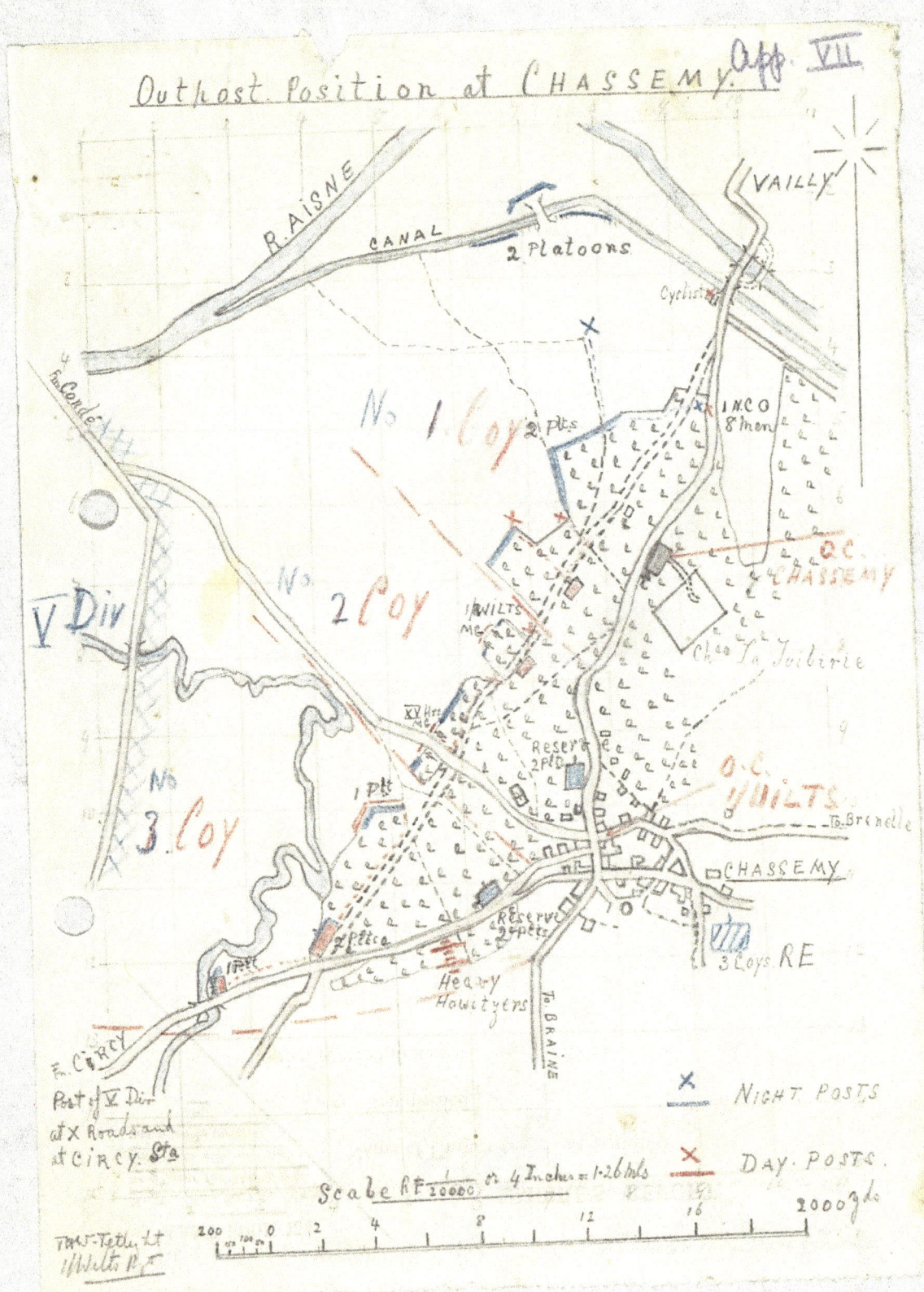

7th Brigade.
3rd Division.

1st BATTALION

THE WILTSHIRE REGIMENT

OCTOBER 1 9 1 4

121/1971

1st Battn Wiltshire Regt.

7th Brigade

Vol III. 1 – 27.10.14

Army Form C. 2118.

WAR DIARY
or
INTELLIGENCE SUMMARY.
(Erase heading not required.)

Instructions regarding War Diaries and Intelligence Summaries are contained in F. S. Regs., Part II. and the Staff Manual respectively. Title pages will be prepared in manuscript.

Hour, Date, Place	Summary of Events and Information	Remarks and references to Appendices
4.30 am. 1st October 1914.	Stood to arms. Relieved in the outpost line by the 3rd Norfolks. Relief effected without drawing fire.	VRT.
6. am. 1st October (Thursday)	Battn. marched by platoons at intervals of 50x from CHASSEMY to AVGY and went into billets at this latter place. The march was concealed by mist.	VRT
9.20 pm. 1st October.	Battn. at 2 hours notice marched to GRAND ROZOY, [march delayed by the 8th Lcy. Bde.]	VRT
3. am. 2nd October 1914. (Friday)	Reached GRAND ROZOY, and went into billets.	VRT.
8.25 pm. 2nd October	Brigade marched to NOROY	VRT.
12.45 am. 3rd October 1914. (Saturday)	Reached NOROY and went into billets	VRT.
7. pm. 3rd October	Brigade marched to VAUMOISE	VRT.
2.15 am. 4th October 1914. (Sunday)	Reached VAUMOISE and went into billets	VRT.
6. pm. 4th October.	Brigade marched to SAINTINES, arrived 11.45 p.m. & into Billets	VRT.
11.45 pm. 5th 4th October	Reached SAINTINES, and went into billets	VRT.
7.30 pm. 5th October (Monday)	Marched from SAINTINES railway station EAST of LE MEUX where Battn. entrained at 10.30 p.m.	VRT.
10.25 pm. 6th October (Tuesday)	Detrained at ABBEVILLE, billeted [at quite a handsome]	VRT.

Army Form C. 2118.

WAR DIARY
or
INTELLIGENCE SUMMARY.
(Erase heading not required.)

Instructions regarding War Diaries and Intelligence Summaries are contained in F.S. Regs. Part II. and the Staff Manual respectively. Title pages will be prepared in manuscript.

Hour, Date, Place	Summary of Events and Information	Remarks and references to Appendices
8.20 a.m. 7th October (Wednesday)	Battn. marched from ABBEVILLE to LA TRIQUERIE CHATEAU where we billeted	W.C.
8th October (Thursday)	Remained at LA TRIQUERIE. A+C Coys found outposts E+W of CHANCY covering the 7th Brigade.	W.C.
1 a.m. 9th October (Friday)	Marched from LA TRIQUERIE in Brigade as rearguard, reached REGNAUVILLE at 7.45 a.m. distance 13 miles.	W.C.
4 p.m. 9th October	Marched from REGNAUVILLE carrying extra 50 rds SAA all Transport but 1 days supplies left behind. Brigade picked up by motor lorries 1 mile S. of HESDIN and motored to PERNES	W.C.
12.30 a.m. 10th October (Saturday)	Arrived PERNES and went into billets. 1st line transport arrived 2.40 p.m. 2nd Lieuts W. de W.H. Bradley and P.E.O. Riddell joined the Battn.	W.C.
9.30 a.m. 11th October (Sunday)	Brigade marched from PERNES and arrived at HINGES at 8.30 p.m. went into billets. B Coy found protective posts.	W.C.
9.30 a.m. 12th October (Monday)	Brigade marched from HINGES to neighbourhood of LA COUTURE where Worcesters, S. Lancs, and R.I.R. became engaged with the enemy along the LEFT bank of the river LOISNE. C Company went in to fill gap between 7th + 8th Brigades and 2nd D Coy went to reinforce the Worcesters but were ordered back about midnight. B Company remained with 42nd Bde R.F.A. as escort.	W.C.

79
3298

Army Form C. 2118.

WAR DIARY
or
INTELLIGENCE SUMMARY.
(Erase heading not required.)

Instructions regarding War Diaries and Intelligence Summaries are contained in F. S. Regs., Part II. and the Staff Manual respectively. Title pages will be prepared in manuscript.

Hour, Date, Place	Summary of Events and Information	Remarks and references to Appendices
1.15 October 1914. (Tuesday)	Battn Brigade advanced across the River LOISNE during the night. Battn Head Quarters moved to EAST entrance to LA COUTURE Village, which was shelled at intervals throughout the day.	J.W.
8.45 pm October 13th	"C" Company returned from the firing line reported 9 killed and 18 wounded.	J.W.P.
14th October 1914. (Wednesday)	"B" Company returned off escort duty to R.F.A. A reinforcement of one Officer (2nd Lt. Gee) and 86 other ranks joined the battalion and were posted A.13, B.16, C.57. Alarm in the firing line at	J.W.
6.10 (pm)	Battn stood to arms, but dismissed about 9.45 (pm). 2 men of "B" Company wounded. Half "A" Coy sent to firing line at night.	J.W.
15th October 1914. (Thursday)	Remained at LA COUTURE. Eleven sick and wounded reported fit.	J.W.P.
16th October 1914. (Friday)	Advanced to NEUF CHAPELLE via RICHEBOURG, relieved S. Lancs in outpost line west of in the BOIS DE BIEZ about 10 p.m. 0 difficult task owing to very dark night.	
17th October 1914. (Saturday)	Brigade advanced in line at 6 a.m. delayed by R.A. Bde on left, halts made LIGNY-LE-GRAND by 10.20 and got in touch with the enemy. Advance continued very slowly, the left always meeting with opposition. The Brigade became very attenuated owing to divergent attacks by the Brigades on our flanks. Entrenched a position at night EAST of LIGNY. LE GRAND. 8 men wounded.	J.W.

WAR DIARY or INTELLIGENCE SUMMARY.

Army Form C. 2118.

(Erase heading not required.)

Instructions regarding War Diaries and Intelligence Summaries are contained in F.S. Regs., Part II. and the Staff Manual respectively. Title pages will be prepared in manuscript.

Hour, Date, Place	Summary of Events and Information	Remarks and references to Appendices
18th October, 1914. (Sunday)	Endeavoured to make found to the front, but enemy appeared to have been strongly reinforced, only succeeded in moving about 200 to 300 yds. Germans shelled trenches and village. Made another effort to get forward at dusk, heavy firing continued till 10.30 p.m., but little progress made. Enemy employed guns, searchlights and star shell, they also fired heavy rifle casualties 2nd Lt. GEE dangerously wounded, 2nd Lt. GASKELL slightly wounded other Ranks 3 killed 21 wounded.	VRT
19th October 1914 (Monday)	"A" + "B" Companies made a little ground. Shell + rifle fire very heavy. 2nd Lt. Lloyd succeeded in making a lodgement with one platoon of D Coy in the outskirts of ILLIES, and was joined by 2nd Lt. Rose with his platoon. At dusk enemy fired a rick close to "B" Coys line which prevented wounded + dead being brought in till late. Rain helped kept the fire down. Enemy used heavy guns during the afternoon. 2nd Lt. Lloyd + Rose withdrawn as their effectual support impossible. Casualties 12 killed and 21 wounded – Capt Stoddart granted The CROIX DE CHEVALIER and O.R. G.M.S. WARWICK, 2. The MEDAILLES MILITAIRES of the LEGION of HONOUR. Special orders of the day received	VRT Appx. VIII

WAR DIARY
or
INTELLIGENCE SUMMARY.
(Erase heading not required.)

Army Form C. 2118.

Instructions regarding War Diaries and Intelligence Summaries are contained in F. S. Regs., Part II. and the Staff Manual respectively. Title pages will be prepared in manuscript.

Hour, Date, Place	Summary of Events and Information	Remarks and references to Appendices
20th October 1914. (Tuesday)	Situation remained unchanged. A+B Coys heavily sniped from the factory entrance.	
21st October 1914. (Wednesday)	Enemy broke through the right of the Brigade line. The line was then broken at dawn behind B Trench, a new position taken. HAZEGARDE. B Company moved off to commence digging. Battalion attacked about 6 p.m. & successfully beat off the enemy.	
22nd October 1914. (Thursday)	Enemy attacked fiercely about 2.30 p.m. and commenced our Retreat (to try the latter cell, held on). Bitter fighting about 2.30 a.m. Oct 4.10 a.m. to heavily to introduce and ASK our new position S.E. from MEPLE & GARDE far in position that afterwards daylight. Trenches in rear of our hill and Grenades out. The German did retire in rear of our hill and commenced now putting up wire entanglements.	
23rd October 1914. (Friday)	Battn. marched at midnight. 'C' Company as rearguard. Moved into position WEST of NEUF CHAPELLE partially prepared by R.E. dug and made down preparing with suitable parapet for troops held. Shall be knock off until attack continued entrenching and afterwards if until dark after dark. Casualties 2 killed 3 wounded the morning blow works.	

WAR DIARY or INTELLIGENCE SUMMARY.

Army Form C. 2118.

Hour, Date, Place	Summary of Events and Information	Remarks and references to Appendices
24 Oct (Sat)	Night attack against trenches started at 12.30 am and continued till about 2.30 am preceded with information of the advance as far as enemy's snipers were permitted. But all troops except the Oxfds out of village by daylight. Shelling of village trenches commenced at 9.45 am. Ceased for few hours & then again continued without a break from 2 to 7 pm. Companies in trenches suffered from shell fire. Then trenches kept clean in dry them heavy shells. Village suffered a good deal. B Coy in dug outs outside village also suffered. Trenches report an attack about 5 pm. Sent up what ammn we could of R Coy to reinforce trenches. 2 Lieut Riddle slightly wounded. 8 men killed, 36 wounded, and 2 or 3 missing. It is feared that most of these men were buried in their dug outs.	about 2–3 am
25 Oct (Sunday)	Moved to Meteren Rest AD further back to what of village. Had D Coy & & Reserve. Trenches shelled pretty hard all day, also HQ a certain amount. Regt on our left had pretty down west of the trenches. Village returned to Meuve provide out up by heavy shellfire. Difficult to get supplies up. Moved HQ up to where open after dark. Relieved A & C Coys in the trenches as soon as possible by B + D Coys also hostilities that remained of the machine gun section, only 2 men left. Some all night. Captain Davis severely wounded. 39 men killed & Lt 2 wounded. 2 Lieut Tetley sent up to take command of A Coy. 2nd Lieut Danis wounded.	
26 Oct (Monday)	Moved HQ back to farm. B + D Coys + 2 platoons A Coy in trenches, 2 platoons A Coy in support. C Coy (80 strong) in reserve. About 1 pm enemy again shelled the trenches and vicinity of HQ very heavily. Regt on our left mostly cleared out of their trenches. At 4.30 pm heard enemy had come through on left of our trenches. Got up to the 2 platoons in support. Bussed up Messine & pressure down, but in time to meet the	

79 / 3328

WAR DIARY or INTELLIGENCE SUMMARY.

Army Form C. 2118.

(Erase heading not required.)

Hour, Date, Place	Summary of Events and Information	Remarks and references to Appendices
29 Oct (Thursday) (Continued)	The Germans advancing from West side of village of NEUVE CHAPELLE. Deployed 2 platoons of C Coy who held them ... at the Rd Queues farm. Enemy came on to within 250 yards on the road in front as it was just getting dusk & proceeded to entrench themselves. Deployed 3 platoons C Coy & attacked them with the bayonet. Drove them back into the turnip fields which killing and wounding a certain number of them. (The ghost) prisoners taken about 6.30 pm he was now informed that 2 Coys S Lan Lancs Regt 2 Coys R Innis Rifle + 2 Coys R Fusiliers were coming up to reinforce us. Arranged for a line to be made and a spread. above the road to clear the wings with the bayonet. Meanwhile C Coy pushes up to the edge of the village. Great delay in getting the line forward. 5 different units his Senior officers to take command. No counter attn after having merely a few for a Regt is on left to come up. The units 1 of 9 R Innis, 2 S Lancs, R I Rifles (5 Coys in all) decided not to wait and had a to relief of their comrades in the trenches. C Coy Wiltshire Regt formed the advanced Guard of the little force, and was led forward by Captain Rosset P.S. Rosson. He advanced into Soundels of to which met with little opposition except from Snipers. Coy Wiltshire Regt pushes on down to left flank of our trenches and the found the adjoining trenches of the R.I.R. Rifles, which had been vacated, and was held by Germans. Cpt Rosson led forward the party with gallantry and attacking the Germans with the bayonet drove them back from the R Irish Rifle trenches. C Coy was occupied this trenches until	

Army Form C. 2118.

WAR DIARY
or
INTELLIGENCE SUMMARY.
(Erase heading not required.)

Hour, Date, Place	Summary of Events and Information	Remarks and references to Appendices

24 Oct. Sunday *continued*

the R. Irish Rifles came up. Rifles had not their trenches and pushed up towards the left. Having seen this part of the task accomplished I (Major Ross) returned to the village where the Brigadier (?) was met. There met the Command Officers and informed them that we were all right in our trenches and Rifles rapidly getting theirs in order, and urged that the above should be most of the line and should be most of the R. Irish Rifles held by the Royal Irish Fusiliers. The O.C. R. Irish Fusiliers this in after O. Irish Rifles, held by the Royal Irish Fusiliers. The Irish Fusiliers had had to fall back in approaching the N. end of NEUVE CHAPELLE village as Battn. came under heavy fire & suffered many casualties. After considerable delay and hesitation as to try and re-establish to bring in the trenches in front of the N end of the village of NEUVE CHAPELLE. It was eventually decided by the senior officer present that to hold the village could not be attacked and cleared without Artillery support, and that to put this he must wait until daylight. All troops were about the line upon which the Royal Fusiliers had been checked. I got to supplies up by hand, also ammunition. It was being rendered impossible by the holes from shell fire. The supplies and ammunition was got down to the trenches. I reinforced the trenches by 50 men of C. Coy. to replace casualties and withdrew almost 3 Offrs to my headquarters in West of village having then left only the headquarters party of about 18 men and 40 men of C. Coy under Captain Richards. There

---

79
3298

WAR DIARY or INTELLIGENCE SUMMARY

Army Form C. 2118.

Hour, Date, Place	Summary of Events and Information	Remarks and references to Appendices
Monday 26 Oct (continued)	During the night 2 Lieutenant I Anderson took a platoon of A Coy (under 2nd Lieut hatten) who O thought had gone up to reinforce the trenches but gotten into touch half the platoon (1+2 men) reported him almost halfway through the village with the object of Establishing Germans in Wind. Working down to find out again getting into the trenches held by the Battalion. The remainder of the platoon were Sgt Hunter was ordered to go back to trenches & he was but is at present to the trenches. Our casualties this day were Captain M.L. Formby Killed. Captain Ikey PS Qnmn dangerously wounded (receiving 2 bullet wounds) he hung to recover some in the Ambulance. This Officer was wounded. Lieut Richardson severely wounded. 20 men killed, 20 men wounded and 10 reported missing.	
Tuesday 27 Oct	Things in at Hd Qtrs seem suspicious to attack against N wing of Bulogs & commencement upon Hq ours deposit it and by daylight of Forces had to were almost surrounded by the enemy. Snipers who has crept up to our trenches were through difficult bone. It was with difficulty we got any communications to and fro. At about 8 am I asked to Regiment HQ without going to the Army, turning the trenches being short. At Brigade at Wolverton state & horses lack it the Telephone Wires. This is ard. No attack having yet being taken. At 11 am the S Lancashire Regt which arrived by my 2 week conference came up to try & reinforce.
6.47 10 am OC R I Rifles in trenches having my front all and enemy had driven his Regt with our but the were retiring as battery came this I immediately reported to Bde H.Q.	

WAR DIARY or INTELLIGENCE SUMMARY

Army Form C. 2118.

(*Erase heading not required.*)

Summary of Events and Information	Remarks and references to Appendices
and about some time receive a message from Bde H.Q. saying Lt Bulfin (acting S Lancashires) would attack the village at 11. a.m.. This attack didnt commence till about noon. and there had been no heavy shot then no where. So before the extreme R Coordination about it. The Coy S Lancashires in my right tested got a bit to attack on to S end of the village. Meanwhile I got a few reports back from our trenches — last message timed 12.15 pm and up to now they appeared to be quite all right. I am informed that a heavy hn and he about 2 p.m. reporting that many appeared to be leaving in an L/F this heavy was now got to be the heaviest being shot. About 3.30 p.m. he noticed British troops returning in our right in a SW direction reinfr'ing the drive from the trenches and last at some time drew a party of 50 to 100 German pushing through. Seeing no sign of pursuit I have now returning. He Coy S Lancashires and one of the Wiltshire Regt who then pursued of the men from the trenches, and returning into the village. Gradually reinforced forwarded to arms for the Qr Mr form. This immediately gave up 150. S Lancashire Regt and to the Wilshire Regt. he checked their advance. And all the off our right flank being exposed to Rrgs trenches were withdrawn to an left rear.	

Army Form C. 2118.

WAR DIARY
or
INTELLIGENCE SUMMARY.
(Erase heading not required.)

Hour, Date, Place	Summary of Events and Information	Remarks and references to Appendices
Tuesday 27th Oct 4 pm	About 4pm 2 Lt Chandler arrived back from the trenches having just been sent to report to Officer i/c his trenches but as he was in large numbers led Coy through to Brig Rifle trenches on our left, manned by a wood near the Chateau at NEUVE CHAPELLE and had then forward to surround and roll up one line of trenches. And that all hope of our being able to hold on there was gone. I immediately communicated this to Bde H.Q. I also in consultation with the O.C. S Lancashire Regt who was with me reported the situation to the R Irish & Lincoln Regt who were in the vicinity. He also said that he did not consider it would be possible for us (S Lancs & Ad Quartn trenches) though in places we were beyond dark and too heavily further instructive forced to, to hold full touch in line with Royal trenches at dusk. I also sent for artillery support regretting him to shell a wood 300 yards to my front where they had been hovering. At about dusk 5.15 pm a message received from Bde said 4/9 Sikhs being sent to your assistance. Held on where we are and counterattack being to to be stopped at 5.35 pm counterattack at present impracticable with help in when we are and see what can be done when 4/7 Sikhs arrive"	

WAR DIARY
INTELLIGENCE SUMMARY.
(Erase heading not required.)

Army Form C. 2118.

Hour, Date, Place	Summary of Events and Information	Remarks and references to Appendices
Tuesday 27th Oct 14	Meanwhile enemy gave up trying to force us and set fire to some corn stacks between us and him and thus illuminated the wire between us, hiding any movement on our part very apparent. 7 pm. No news of 47th Sikhs. Officer B.P. Brown Staff came to see situation. He informed me that he thought 47th Sikhs had been diverted elsewhere. but that 9th Bhopal Infantry were coming up on our right. About 7.45 pm received a message from O.C. R. Fusiliers (Senior Officer in vicinity) ordering me to take up a different position. Arrangements were made to entrench. Many casualties the situation, i.e. that our forward position was in advance of two pontoon lines to be in hopes that we could not entrench under the light of the enemy's fires, that a letter full of fire and practice were to be returned by falling back 300 yards to his left to R Fusiliers to be of the essential Regt Myself went back & saw O.C. R Fusiliers who agreed not now to withdraw. At 9 pm seeing a strong enemy party in front with the enemy we got back and entrenched a line 300 to 400 yards to rear, in prolongation of the R Fusiliers line. Before this was ready to receive information that the line would be taken over by 47th Sikhs who had been dead [?] for and by 2 Coys Indian Sappers Miners.	

WAR DIARY
INTELLIGENCE SUMMARY

Wednesday 28th Oct

He had meanwhile established trench work the 9th Bhopal Infantry on his right. About 1 am he occupied the line he prepared. At about 2 am 2 coys 34 Pioneers arrived and began relieving the men in the line, about this time a good deal of firing took place. About the Sapper & Miners Land (where was [Lt-Colonel] Hill) withdrew to covering party under Capt Hore, and as he the left the firing at German trenches i.e. he had withdrew to PONT LOGY. When he was ordered to remain at Lt Anglesmur ——— and Lt Strachan he would be permitted to return to RICHBOURG St VAAST. Reached PONT LOGY about 3 am. A good deal of firing going on in front and heavy bullets coming down the road in which he was supposed to halt. After a short time he got Regt (by this time he had collected about another 120 men who got away from the trenches) into an enclosure which gave protection from these stray bullets and gave to him a chance of a rest. At about 6.30 an [order] was sent for the 2nd bd to attack the enemy round the NEUVE CHAPELLE this morning and tho' he wanted the Regt to what was ready of it to support the attack. We stood by ready by manning last ditch for their Armament at about 9 am he received orders to proceed to billets at RICHBOURG ST VAAST which he reached at 10 am. Marching in were 5 Officers + about 200 men. At RICHBOURG he found ready for us the 6th Reinforcement & 83 rank + file under

Captain Guy B. Renard

WAR DIARY or INTELLIGENCE SUMMARY.

Army Form C. 2118.

Hour, Date, Place	Summary of Events and Information	Remarks and references to Appendices
Wednesday 28 Oct 1914	On arrival in billets he tried to estimate our casualties for the forenoon day the 27th Oct. And the NCO sent in was as follows. Killed. Captain T.W. Stoddart and 30 men. Wounded 2nd Lieutenant BRADLEY and 120 men. Missing Lieutenants Oliphant, Ward-Tetley, 2nd Lieutenants Rose, Riley, Lloyd, Watson, and Hunter. (all of which are believed to have been taken prisoners) and about 150 men. Note [As to above account is as seen by me, who could not see the action round to Trenches. At this time his men reached I am sorry to attach an account from some of the NCOs who got back from the trenches.] (attached as Appendix IX) At 2 pm Regt ordered not to take up a line covering RICHBOURG to the East, as this had been time to rearrange front to last reinforcement he forwarded out as 8 coys each of about 100 men. The reinforcement found a company by Remarks, under Capt Gary Renaud. He hurried up this line Hautbourdin at 5.6.5 pm he received an order to proceed across country and go at once to assistance of 2nd Cavalry Brigade who were holding the trenches about PONT LOGY. Arrived at PONT LOGY at 6.6.5 pm, as after arrival there he asked to find. 50 men to reinforce 9 Lancers. Who had been dismounted forward Send up Capt Gary Renaud and 50 men. The draft to reinforce 9 Lancers Remains bivouaced in a field close by a very cold night	

WAR DIARY or INTELLIGENCE SUMMARY

Army Form C. 2118.

Hour, Date, Place	Summary of Events and Information	Remarks and references to Appendices
Thursday 29th Octr 1914	Returned to trenches at RICHBOURG ST VAAST with the 2nd Cav Regt, the line held by them having been taken over by infantry during the night. Reorganised Battn into 3 Coys A.C. & D. until further orders. Received a large consignment of mail warm clothing and gifts from friends at home towards Xmas. Village of RICHBOURG shelled by Germans about 3 p.m. the first few shells falling in our billeting area. Obtained permission from Major Rotton in C.O. of Troops in LA COUTURE which was shelling but slightly also from up Rotton about 1 mile W.S.W RICHBOURG keeping it extended so as to minimise loss in case of further shelling. At dusk and like party to remove our equipment and stores when I received an order to proceed to LA COUTURE and to find billets there, this we did getting into billets about 8 p.m. a hot night of further shelling. At the time he received an order to proceed to fighting continued along our front all night, and moving again shelled RICHBOURG during the night. Casualties. 2 killed 21 wounded and also 2 horses	
Friday 30th Octr 1914	Stood by waiting for orders, which we got about 1 p.m. we marched at 2.30 p.m. in a N.W. direction through LESTREM, LA GORGUE, ESTAIRES & DOULIEU where we halted into billets for the night.	
Saturday 31st Octr 1914	Marched at 9 a.m. to MERRIS. When it was found that there was not sufficient billeting accommodation for the Brigade. The Battalion was in consequence sent out to NORD-HELP about a mile N. of there. Here we got into billets in one scattered farms. But baggage wagons up. Was informed our Brigade HQ. was which I got a meal here and got instructions accordingly	C. Rich head Lt Col C. C. Wiltshire Regt

WAR DIARY or INTELLIGENCE SUMMARY

Army Form C. 2118.

Hour, Date, Place	Summary of Events and Information	Remarks and references to Appendices
Tuesday 27th Oct 1914 Appendix IX	Appendix IX Account of the action on Tuesday 27th Oct by NCO from the Trenches. 2nd Lieut C Chandler, 1st Wiltshire Regt. who was near the left flank of the trenches held by the Regt states:- The line of trenches held by the R Irish Rifles on our left was vacated by that Regt. by 10 a.m. and those trenches were shortly afterwards occupied by Germans. Our trenches were kept forward for some time, but a steady fire kept up from the front. About 11 am our trenches were reinforced by supports unknown to hand. Pottery & 2nd Lieut Martin. At 12.15 pm I reported to HdQre that he had suffisient men in the trenches and that we were holding our own. (Note this is last message or letter received from the trenches) About 2 pm he became aware that the enemy had forced through to his trenches previously held by the R Irish Rifles and delivered a crossed near to CHATEAU which was hard. About 10 mins later they debrys from here in about 10 or more lines and proceeded to roll up the line of our trenches from our left flank. The enemy were also holding the VILLAGE of NEUVE CHAPELLE about 200 yards in rear of us.	

WAR DIARY
or
INTELLIGENCE SUMMARY.
(Erase heading not required.)

Army Form C. 2118.

Hour, Date, Place	Summary of Events and Information	Remarks and references to Appendices

Thursday 29th Oct

After discussing the situation with the Chief Officers forward, he decided that he must give way, and had further assistance in our forward position was not possible. He passed down to our right along to this of our trenches and getting not formed a line in open facing to emerge forward movement. There was some delay in getting out of the trenches as Capt Stewart (the Senior Officer in the trenches) refused to move till he saw the order for himself. When he decided that to two Coast Attack. The Boers in getting through to this here heavy. He now permitted our right in the left of this still hold by the Royal West Kent Regt and formed a line to cover this flank and stay to intercept advance. About 3.15 pm having ser that another of the forward position out like the Peak had got through, Col Hand Tetley told me to go myself and inform the OC Posts that I was getting to him about 4.15 ordered our a withdrawal rate, the money being cut from there between us and our headquarters and reserve Company

WAR DIARY or INTELLIGENCE SUMMARY

Army Form C. 2118.

Hour, Date, Place	Summary of Events and Information	Remarks and references to Appendices
Thursday 29 Oct 1914	Sergt A J Postman C Coy 1st Battalion. I remonstrated about 2/Lt Chandler he said. I remained with Captain Stewart, who together with Major Buckle, but Rates[?] proved to be covering the huts Rates' Flank. 2 Lts Lloyd, Orr, + Riley were being D Coy. were having a form in the line he had taken up. Captn Stewart had about about dusk, three of the wounds shortly afterwards he was in to this line till about 10 pm. When we were relieved by a company R W Kents and some Indian Regt. Shortly afterwards we were ordered to report our our Battalion headquarters. from to time the many wounded on flank we were fighting at close quarters, almost up to the time we were relieved. Our men having to bayonet on several occasions. An attempt was made to recover our men from being to the Joy was by a bayonet charge but only about 15 to 20 yds of the heavy [wounded?] got back without having R W etc &c wounded.	
	On the fighting round NEUVE CHAPELLE from the 23 to 29th Oct 1914 it is estimated that the casualties were Officers killed 2, wounded 5, missing 7 = total 14 Officers Rank & file " 459 " 153 " 150 = " 350 Rank & file	to above is only our approximate

T Broke Whyt
OC 1st Ba Middlesex Regt 29/10/14

8

7th Bde (3rd Div) — 1st Bn Wiltshire Regt

Date	Officers Killed	Officers Wounded	Officers Missing	Other Ranks Killed	Other Ranks Wounded	Other Ranks Missing
13. 10. 14				3	14	
14. 10. 14					2	
15. 10. 14					1	
16. 10. 14					8	
17. 10. 14				1	21	
18. 10. 14				12	20	
19. 10. 14		2/Lt A.M. Lee		3	8 12	
20. 10. 14		" G.H. Jackell			5	
21. 10. 14						
22. 10. 14				2	3	
23. 10. 14						

Date	Officers			Other Ranks		
	Killed	Wounded	Missing	Killed	Wounded	Missing
1st Jun?				25	94	23
21.10.14		2nd Lt P.W. Russell		7	38	
25.10.14		Capt H.R.W. Bruere		37	42	
26.10.14	Capt M.K. Kennedy	Capt R.L. Houston Lt E.H.B. Richardson		20	40	10
27.1.14	Sgt 7105 Stidston	2/Lt Ord Wilmer Hobart F.R.O. Oliphant Bradley	2/Lt 1911? O Giffard H.B. Rose H.W. Clegg M.K. Wotton T.H. Riley W. Martin	27	120	
29.10.14					4	1
					160	

7th Brigade.

3rd Division.

1st BATTALION

THE WILTSHIRE REGIMENT

NOVEMBER 1 9 1 4

Nov 7/3

121/2590

121/2590

P1. Casualties in detail to 4th Nov — interesting as to wastage statistics.

7th Brigade

1st Wiltshire Regt.

Vol IV. 1 — 30.11.14

first month forwarded
previously

Army Form C. 2118.

WAR DIARY
or
INTELLIGENCE SUMMARY.
(Erase heading not required.)

Instructions regarding War Diaries and Intelligence Summaries are contained in F.S. Regs., Part II. and the Staff Manual respectively. Title pages will be prepared in manuscript.

Hour, Date, Place	Summary of Events and Information	Remarks and references to Appendices
Sunday 1st November 1914	Had a Muster parade to try and ascertain that our exact numbers were 12 noon got orders to be prepared to move. Strength return showed 9 Officers & 48 ranks & file Captain Thruston (Adjt Royal Irish Rifles) and Lt Carrington who were wounded 26/8/14 reported. Rested. Also 2nd Lieut Down 2nd Bn R. Ir. R. and 110 men making the 1st Reinforcement arrived for duty with 1st Battalion. Marched at 1pm through BAILLEUL, which was very congested with troops and traffic to LOCRE when we arrived at 6pm and went into billets [LOCRE is about 1 mile inside the BELGIUM frontier] being ordered to frontier about 5pm on the way.	
Monday 2nd November 1914 LOCRE BELGIUM	Strength return. Taking in draft. Received yesterday bring us up to 13 Officers – 521 Other ranks. Day spent in cleaning up & getting rifles etc in working condition. Got 2 forms received. Orders to stand by "ready" to go to the assistance of the French troops about WYTSCHAETE, E. of hd. Believed to show up in White smocks room for French troops. We have not sent out.	
Tuesday 3rd November 1914 LOCRE	Lieut Or hr Hewitt 2nd Bn Wiltshire Regt came in with the train of the 2nd Battn and he gave us a certain amount of information as to their condition. And the identity of our return in which they lost heavily in Sir I. on 24th Oct 1914. Sergt Arnold + Corpl Lawton by F.G.C. Martial. Nothing of any importance occurred. Lieut B. H. Goodwin performed the duties of Acting Adjt to the Battn from 28 Oct to 3/Nov inclusive vice Capt Pest P.S. Cowan wounded. Sent diary for Oct off by post original to DAG Base duplicate to OC Depot.	1B

WAR DIARY
or
INTELLIGENCE SUMMARY.
(Erase heading not required.)

Army Form C. 2118.

Hour, Date, Place	Summary of Events and Information	Remarks and references to Appendices
Wednesday 4th Nov. 1914 LOCRE	Halted at LOCRE. Battalion resumed to hold itself in readiness to support the if required. Lieut G.S. Bourne assumed the duties of Acty Adjutant to the Battn. vice Bowen wounded.	
Thursday 5th Nov 1914 HOOGE	There had a rough estimate of our casualties since the campaign started. We in first 3 months, what I attach. It shews that we have practically lost or temporary hors de Combat, 26 Officers and 1000 men. A copy of the special order of the day dated 2 Nov/14 by Lt C. Portich Army is attached. Marched 6am to DICKEBUSH halted in field till 4pm roads very muddy and congested with traffic left 4pm marched to HOOGE via YPRES where we relieved of 20th Bde. Battalion was put in Reserve in "dug outs" in a wood. 1 Wounded	4/11/14
Friday 6th Nov 1914 HOOGE	Reserve in "dug outs". Little shelling. Party went out after daylight but could not find or them small attacks on Jerry line but not determined	
Saturday 7th Nov HOOGE	Very foggy weather heavy firing on left slight shelling mostly Shrapnell. D & A Companys relieved Gordon Highlanders in firing line C company staying in reserve	

Army Form C. 2118.

WAR DIARY
or
INTELLIGENCE SUMMARY.
(Erase heading not required.)

Instructions regarding War Diaries and Intelligence Summaries are contained in F. S. Regs., Part II. and the Staff Manual respectively. Title pages will be prepared in manuscript.

Hour, Date, Place	Summary of Events and Information	Remarks and references to Appendices
Sunday 8th Nov. HOOGE	2 Companys in trenches, quiet morning up to midday when heavy shelling commenced but fairly quiet Our trenches Germans attacked night of 9th 10th. It is found that dug outs are useless against high explosive and common shell but are good protection from shrapnel and the Wounded	Bldy
Monday 9th Nov. HOOGE.	Foggy morning. Made more "Dug outs" in wood. Fairly quiet morning. Relieved by Gordon Highlanders Two wounded.	Bldy
Tuesday 10th Nov. HOOGE	Foggy morning. Shelling started early and continued heavy till 10am then 2/2nd and after that intermittals till dark night. Be Wounded	Bldy
Wednesday 11th Nov. HOOGE	Enemy started to shell at 6.20am and continued on and off all day. Germans were said to be massing in front of our line but nothing came of it owing to our artillery fire. 2nd Coy relieved Gordons about midnight a very wet night. 7th Bde supported 15 Bde A Coy	Bldy

WAR DIARY
or
INTELLIGENCE SUMMARY.
(Erase heading not required.)

Army Form C. 2118.

Hour, Date, Place	Summary of Events and Information	Remarks and references to Appendices
Thursday 12th HOOGE In trenches	A Coy stayed with 15th Bde. Enemy shelled a good deal during the day; but did not make an infantry attack. Four wounded.	BM 6 2
Friday 13th HOOGE In trenches	Enemy shelled steadily our guns replying. German brought up a gun. Our dead ground to within 100ᵡ of our trenches. Grenade attacked in the afternoon against the St Lancs were found back (there were on our right) their trenches were retaken at dusk. A Coy rejoined from 15th Bde. Gordons delivered firing line about 12 midnight. Three killed six wounded.	BM
Saturday 14th HOOGE In trenches	Fairly quiet morning slight rain. Took 1½ to support 9th Bde. Considerable shelling in the afternoon culminating in an attack on Gordons who were in the front line, but were driven back. Two killed & wounded one missing	BM

WAR DIARY
or
INTELLIGENCE SUMMARY.
(Erase heading not required.)

Army Form C. 2118.

Hour, Date, Place	Summary of Events and Information	Remarks and references to Appendices
15th November HOOGE	Made M.Gun trench from which to support the firing line. Attack against firing line repulsed. Started snowing. Germans shelling at intervals three companies relieved the 9th Div we have now taken over the whole of the sector, the other two regiments of the Brigade being greatly reduced in officers and men. The th trenches were very wet, heavy musketry between at 12 and Rear.	62 am 10ry
16th November. HOOGE	In trenches. Germans continued to snipe towards our centre. Heavy shelling. 2 killed 3 wounded.	10ry
17th November HOOGE	Shelling started about 9am. Infantry attack at noon. about 150 Germans got into B Coys advanced trenches at 12.10 a platoon of D Company executed a bayonet charge against them, and drove them out killing about 58 Germans and wounding many others. They then started to shell D Company very heavily also using a mortar	10ry

WAR DIARY or INTELLIGENCE SUMMARY

(Erase heading not required.)

Army Form C. 2118.

Hour, Date, Place	Summary of Events and Information	Remarks and references to Appendices
17th November HOOGE	Major Roche killed & still an Lt Goodhart took over duty of adjutant. Capt Brown dangerously wounded Seriously wounded 2nd Lt killed by bullet wound 11 killed 60 wounded	BM
18th November HOOGE	Major Roche buried 200° NE of Chateau S of MENIN-YPRES road near HOOGE. Dug new trench E of wood for use under shell fire. German killed lately. 10 Boys moved out into little wood E of ☓ Many Aeroplanes. Cold and wet.	BM
19th November HOOGE	Very bad weather. Foraging hard work now. Germans shelled in morning afternoon quiet. Relieved by Gordons about 9pm (killed no Cheshires left of our line) about midnight. Many hostile aeroplanes. 3 killed 12 Wounded	62 mm BM

WAR DIARY
or
INTELLIGENCE SUMMARY.
(Erase heading not required.)

Army Form C. 2118.

Hour, Date, Place	Summary of Events and Information	Remarks and references to Appendices
20th November HOOGE	Fine day, but very cold. Germans shelled off and on but did not do much damage. Relieved by French troops relief completed by 10 a.m. 3 killed & 12 wounded.	
21st November WESTOUTRE	Relayed on road at HOOGE shelled by light shrapnel between HOOGE and YPRES causing considerable consternation. Marched to WESTOUTRE via VLAMERTINGHE which place was reached about 8.30 am about 12 miles very trying march after 15 days in the trenches, delayed by transport on the road. Went into billets and spent day clearing up. 3 killed 21 wounded.	

WAR DIARY
or
INTELLIGENCE SUMMARY.
(Erase heading not required.)

Army Form C. 2118.

Hour, Date, Place	Summary of Events and Information	Remarks and references to Appendices
22nd November WESTOUTRE	[Church Parade] Draft of 91 arrived and were posted to Coys.	BM
23rd November	2nd Lt Emmett & 2nd Lt Green joined Battalion. Training under Company Arrangement	BM
24th November	Rest & reorganization	BM / BM
25th November	Rest & reorganization	BM
26th November	Rest & reorganization & [Field Marshall Sir John French spoke to the Battalion on their recent achievements.]	BM
27th November	Marched at 5.15 pm to SCHERPENBERG went into Billets (indifferent)	BM
28th November SCHERPENBERG	Rest.	BM
29th November	[Church Parade 10 am] Rest Company Commanders reconnoitred position ahead KEMMEL	BM

WAR DIARY
or
INTELLIGENCE SUMMARY.

(Erase heading not required.)

Army Form C. 2118.

Hour, Date, Place	Summary of Events and Information	Remarks and references to Appendices
30th November	Marched to SCHERPENBERG to trenches in front of KEMEL. Relieved Lincolns relief finished at 8 pm with 3 Coys in firing line	BEF
1st December BEF		62

Army Form C. 2118.

WAR DIARY
or
INTELLIGENCE SUMMARY.
(Erase heading not required.)

Hour, Date, Place	Summary of Events and Information	Remarks and references to Appendices
	Rough estimate of our wastage since the beginning of this campaign (3 months since receipt of order to mobilise).	
Went into field with arose up to 23 Sept 14	Officers 27 Rank & file - 977 " 10 " 380	(Casualties Officers killed Capt Bowie, Lt Rawson. Casualties replacements, wounded Lt Hart Capt Rowan, Lt Bowie, also injured Compton Rowan, Capt Hue + 2 others slightly wounded return report are not included.)
1 Reinforcement up to 4 Nov.	19 617 13 550	
Arose in action prior up to 1st Nov 1914	30 1167 16 640	Casualties Officers Killed. Capt Bartlett. Formby Lt Linville wounded Capt. Rowan Burns, Lt Richardson, Lt Barkdoll Missing Lilwin Forremeille Alphent, Lent Kelly, Lt Bar, Lloyd Riley Watson Martin
Return	14 - 527	Invalided sick 2 Stewart Linnell Hewitt total 16
	Present state Aeres 14 Officers which Richard officers 521 rank + file	
	Total wastage up to date in first 3 months appear to be 96 Officers and 1000 men or practically a whole Battn.	
a) includes Capt Rowan Lt Bowie Lt Carrington "Returned from being wounded"		

Newhayer
OC 1 R. Warwick

7th Brigade.
3rd Division.

1st BATTALION

THE WILTSHIRE REGIMENT

DECEMBER 1 9 1 4

121/3771

7th Brigade

1st Batt'n Wiltshire Reg't.

Vol V. 1 — 31.12.14

Army Form C. 2118.

WAR DIARY
or
INTELLIGENCE SUMMARY.
(Erase heading not required.)

Instructions regarding War Diaries and Intelligence Summaries are contained in F.S. Regs., Part II. and the Staff Manual respectively. Title pages will be prepared in manuscript.

Hour, Date, Place	Summary of Events and Information	Remarks and references to Appendices
1st December KEMMEL	Quiet day hardly any shelling slight musketry attack 7 at 5 p.m. but it did not materialise	Bty
2nd December KEMMEL	Quiet day no shelling desultory rifle fire after dark. Royal Lieut. to Officers came to reconnoitre position. 2nd Lt Lloyd awarded D.S.O.	Bty 62
3rd December KEMMEL WESTOUTRE	(Our own) Quiet day. Heavy gun fire on right at 2 p.m. lasting 10 minutes. Relieved by Royal Scots relief completed at 7 p.m. Marched to WESTOUTRE [went into billets at 10 p.m.]	Bty

WAR DIARY
or
INTELLIGENCE SUMMARY.

(Erase heading not required.)

Army Form C. 2118.

Hour, Date, Place	Summary of Events and Information	Remarks and references to Appendices
4th December WESTOUTRE	Rest & Reorganisation	BM
5th December WESTOUTRE	Rest & Reorganisation. Telephone class formed. Very wet day.	BM
6th December LOCRE.	Voluntary service 10 am. 3 pm Marched to LOCRE and went into Billets. Draft of 111 arrived (80 KA & 31 discharged from Hospital	BM
7th December LOCRE	Interior Economy. Lt Col Hasted rejoined Battalion. Very wet day & night.	BM
8th December LOCRE	Inspection of Battalion. Horses, kettles etc by C.O. 7.30 pm Battalion marched to KEMMEL and went into Reserve to 9th Brigade uneventful night	BM

WAR DIARY
or
INTELLIGENCE SUMMARY.
(Erase heading not required.)

Army Form C. 2118.

Hour, Date, Place	Summary of Events and Information	Remarks and references to Appendices
9th December In trenches near KEMMEL	During KEMMEL at 6.15am the Battalion less C & A Coys returned to billets at LOCRE which was reached at 7am. Stayed at LOCRE till 3pm marched to position on left of 4th Bde in front of KEMMEL. Relieved Lincolns by 6pm. Trenches in a very wet condition. A quiet night. Rain at intervals all day. 1 killed (accident)	BHQ
10th December In trenches near KEMMEL	A quiet day. Germans shelled after midday, falling near 4th Bde H.Q. pressing stations, but no damage done. There was heavy firing on our left on the French lines. Wet day.	BHQ
11th December In trenches near KEMMEL	5.30am – 6.30am very heavy gun fire probably French about 5–7 miles on our left, mainly morning and just day our guns fired during afternoon which was hardly replied to. Lt. Colley joined Battalion.	BHQ
12th December LOCRE	A quiet night. Enemy shelled during the morning but the majority of the shells did not explode. Relieved by Liverpool Scottish by 6.30pm and returned to LOCRE	BHQ

Army Form C. 2118.

WAR DIARY
INTELLIGENCE SUMMARY.
(Erase heading not required.)

Hour, Date, Place	Summary of Events and Information	Remarks and references to Appendices
13th November. LOCRE.	Rest. Fine day, rain at night	BM
14th November. LOCRE.	Battalion stood to arms at 7.45am and remained under arms till 10am. Had orders for rest of day to be ready to turn out at short notice. Dull day, rain at night.	BM
15th December In trenches near KEMMEL	Stood to arms at 4 am. Left LOCRE at 3pm and marched via KEMMEL to the trenches. Relieved Liverpool Scottish without incident. One Company in Support and one in Reserve & rest each amount of sniping otherwise was quiet. Dull and wet day.	BM
16th December In trenches near KEMMEL	Enemy shells dropped in rear of our trenches in the afternoon, many of them did not go off. Engagement made with the French on our left to improve the communication between our left and their right. Company in front were relieved by support reserve company & this again fires each Company in turn & the night in 3 in Reserve	BM Capt Miller Wounded 3 Other Ranks "

WAR DIARY
or
INTELLIGENCE SUMMARY.

(Erase heading not required.)

Army Form C. 2118.

Instructions regarding War Diaries and Intelligence Summaries are contained in F. S. Regs., Part II. and the Staff Manual respectively. Title pages will be prepared in manuscript.

Hour, Date, Place	Summary of Events and Information	Remarks and references to Appendices
17th December Trenches near KEMMEL	Bombardment of Enemy by French Howitzers at 10am good shooting. Germans reply intermittently throughout the day but did no damage. Work done on communication with the French and a section put to watch the gap. A good deal of sniping throughout the day and night. Fair weather.	RAG
18th December Trenches near KEMMEL	Heavy bombardments by our guns at intervals throughout the day only slight reply by Germans. Relieved by Middlesex & R.D.C. over our lines and part of the 1st Rifle Brigade successfully finished 10pm. Marched to LOCRE. Draft of 110 arrived. Fair weather.	RAG
19th December LOCRE	Rest, Reorganisation, Interior Economy.	RAG
20th December LOCRE	Rest, Interior Economy	RAG

Army Form C. 2118.

WAR DIARY
or
INTELLIGENCE SUMMARY.
(Erase heading not required.)

Instructions regarding War Diaries and Intelligence Summaries are contained in F. S. Regs., Part II. and the Staff Manual respectively. Title pages will be prepared in manuscript.

Hour, Date, Place	Summary of Events and Information	Remarks and references to Appendices
21st December LOCRE	Rest	BM
22nd December LOCRE	Rest	BM
23rd December LOCRE	Rest	BM
24th December In trenches near KEMMEL	Marched from LOCRE at 3.15 pm and proceeded via KEMMEL to the section of trenches known as J took over from Northumberland Fusiliers completed by 8.30 pm night spent improving trenches 1 killed 2 wounded	BM
25th December In trenches near KEMMEL.	Attack fog all day practically no shelling on either side but a little sniping in the trenches. The same system is in vogue in the trenches i.e. One company in fire trenches, one in support and one in reserve. Owing to moon-light a good deal of difficulty in relieving fire trenches. Cold. 2 killed 1 wounded 1 missing	BM

Army Form C. 2118.

WAR DIARY
or
INTELLIGENCE SUMMARY.
(Erase heading not required.)

Instructions regarding War Diaries and Intelligence Summaries are contained in F.S. Regs., Part II. and the Staff Manual respectively. Title pages will be prepared in manuscript.

Hour, Date, Place	Summary of Events and Information	Remarks and references to Appendices
26th December In trenches near KEMMEL	Germans did a good deal of shelling but most of their shells did not burst. A good deal of sniping in trenches. Cold & frost. 2 killed 1 wounded.	
27th December In trenches near KEMMEL	Germans shelled near trenches and also near LAITERIE where reserve company is situated but did no damage again many of the shells did not burst. Throughout the time the Battalion has been in these trenches the work of improvement has been going on. Now the trenches are fairly habitable. Relieved by (2nd) Middlesex by 8.30 p.m. and marched to billets in WESTOUTRE the day was cold and windy. 1 killed 1 wounded 2 missing	
28th December WESTOUTRE	Rest.	

Army Form C. 2118.

WAR DIARY
or
INTELLIGENCE SUMMARY.
(Erase heading not required.)

Instructions regarding War Diaries and Intelligence Summaries are contained in F. S. Regs., Part II. and the Staff Manual respectively. Title pages will be prepared in manuscript.

Hour, Date, Place	Summary of Events and Information	Remarks and references to Appendices
BH 29th December WESTOUTRE	Rest	BH
30th December WESTOUTRE	Rest	BH
31st December LOCRE	Marched from WESTOUTRE at 4 p.m. got into Billets at LOCRE at 5 p.m.	BH

3RD DIVISION
7TH INFY BDE

1ST BATTALION
WILTSHIRE REGT.
JAN-OCT 1915.

To 7 BDE 25 DIV

7th Inf.Bde.
3rd Div.

WAR DIARY

1st BATTN. THE WILTSHIRE REGIMENT.

J A N U A R Y

1 9 1 5

WAR DIARY
or
INTELLIGENCE SUMMARY.

(Erase heading not required.)

Army Form C. 2118.

Instructions regarding War Diaries and Intelligence Summaries are contained in F.S. Regs., Part II. and the Staff Manual respectively. Title pages will be prepared in manuscript.

Hour, Date, Place	Summary of Events and Information	Remarks and references to Appendices
1st January LOCRE	Rest	Bty
2nd January LOCRE	Rest	Bty
3rd January LOCRE	Rest	Bty
4th January In trenches near KEMMEL	Moved at 4 pm to section of the trenches known as J. took over from 5th Dublins relief carried out by 8 pm 2 men wounded.	Bty
5th January In trenches near KEMMEL	An uneventful day handed over trenches known as J5.6.7.8.9 and J5 to 6 8th Bde & five day slight rain towards evening & very quiet day	Bty
6th January In trenches near KEMMEL	A considerable amount of shelling at our guns and along main road no damage appeared to be done, a fair day rain at night. Lt Caron joined Battalion	Bty
7th January In trenches near KEMMEL	A considerable amount of shelling at our guns which were more active than usual trenches in a very wet condition, heavy rain 1 man wounded	Bty

Army Form C. 2118.

WAR DIARY
or
INTELLIGENCE SUMMARY.
(Erase heading not required.)

Instructions regarding War Diaries and Intelligence Summaries are contained in F. S. Regs., Part II. and the Staff Manual respectively. Title pages will be prepared in manuscript.

Hour, Date, Place	Summary of Events and Information	Remarks and references to Appendices
8th January. LOCRE	A quiet day, snipers very active during day. Lt 6th [Queens?] relieved by 5th [Dublins?] by 8.30 p.m. marched to billets at LOCRE & shortly day. 1 man killed. 1 wounded.	BAy
9th January LOCRE	Rest.	BAy
10th January LOCRE	Rest	BAy
11th January LOCRE	Rest	BAy
12th January In trenches near KEMMEL	Marched from LOCRE to J section of trenches in front of KEMMEL. Relieved 5th [Dublins?] the system to one company in firing line and support the ½ Coy local reserve by night only.	BAy
13th January In trenches near KEMMEL	A fairly quiet day, snipers busy as usual. 1 man wounded	BAy
14th January In trenches near KEMMEL	Quiet day, nothing of note occurred. 1 man killed.	BAy

WAR DIARY or INTELLIGENCE SUMMARY.

(Erase heading not required.)

Instructions regarding War Diaries and Intelligence Summaries are contained in F. S. Regs., Part II. and the Staff Manual respectively. Title pages will be prepared in manuscript.

Hour, Date, Place	Summary of Events and Information	Remarks and references to Appendices
15th January In trenches near KEMMEL	Heavy rifle and gun fire kept up by no at 9 pm enemy did not reply. Any approach resented. 1 man killed.	Ay
16th January In trenches near KEMMEL LOCRE	A quiet day. A farm just in rear of Battalion Head quarters took fire and the enemy put some shrapnel over presumably at the smoke. Relieved about 4 p.m. by 5th Fusiliers. Returned to Billets at LOCRE. 2 other ranks killed. 1 Wounded. draft of 150 joined Battalion	Bay
17th January In trenches near KEMMEL LOCRE	Rest	Bay
18th January LOCRE	Rest.	Bay
19th January LOCRE	Rest.	Bay
20th January LOCRE In trenches near KEMMEL	Marched to J section of the trenches and took over from 5th Fusiliers. Trenches in shocking state.	
21st January In trenches near KEMMEL	A quiet day, some shelling in the afternoon by KEMMEL. Trenches improved.	

INTELLIGENCE SUMMARY.

WAR DIARY
or
INTELLIGENCE SUMMARY.
(Erase heading not required.)

Instructions regarding War Diaries and Intelligence Summaries are contained in F. S. Regs., Part II. and the Staff Manual respectively. Title pages will be prepared in manuscript.

Hour, Date, Place	Summary of Events and Information	Remarks and references to Appendices
22nd January In trenches near KEMMEL	Heavy shell fire round trenches at 12 noon and Ypres, no damage done. Intermous sniping throughout the day.	BM
23rd January In trenches near KEMMEL	Heavy shell fire from S.E. believed to be 6" howitzers at 12 noon and 4 hrs trenches damaged. Continuous rifle fire on our left throughout the night. Casualties 8 killed 4 wounded	BM
24th January In trenches near KEMMEL LOCRE	Heavy shell fire from same direction at 10.30am and 4.30pm trenches slightly damaged. Relieved at 7pm by 5th Fusiliers and marched to billets at LOCRE. 1 man wounded.	BM
25th January LOCRE	Rest	BM
26th January LOCRE	Rest	BM
27 January LOCRE	Rest 2/Lt Webber and draft of 128 joined Battalion	BM

WAR DIARY
or
INTELLIGENCE SUMMARY.

(Erase heading not required.)

Instructions regarding War Diaries and Intelligence Summaries are contained in F.S. Regs., Part II. and the Staff Manual respectively. Title pages will be prepared in manuscript.

Hour, Date, Place	Summary of Events and Information	Remarks and references to Appendices
28th January In trenches near KEMMEL	Marched to the same sector of trenches at 4.30 p.m. and took over from 5th Fusiliers. Very bright moon but relief carried out without incident. Trenches much improved. Frosty night. 1 man killed.	[signature]
29th January In trenches near KEMMEL	A clear bright day, several aeroplanes about. Telephone both ways traced up. Heavy shelling but KEMMEL being cleared of good deal of rifle fire all night. 1 man killed. Frosty night.	[signature]
30th January In trenches near KEMMEL	Trenches shelled by enemy but no damage. Continuous sniping all day. Snowy night. 2 men wounded. Cold.	[signature]
31st January In trenches near KEMMEL	Trenches shelled slightly but no damage. Continuous sniping, snowing which died away at [illegible]. 1 man killed.	[signature]

K19 N14

WAR DIARY
or
INTELLIGENCE SUMMARY.
(Erase heading not required.)

Summary of Events and Information	Remarks and references to Appendices

Notes on the Operations during the last month

The weather on the whole has been bad and the condition of the trenches has at times been of the worst. Broad and the latter end of the month owing to better weather conditions and also to the ever supply of material and the experience gained, the condition of the trenches has been much improved. The attached sketch shows roughly the type of trench used, but trenches vary with the condition of ground and the material asked is available. Pumps have been found of the greatest value for keeping the water in the trenches under control. Sumps pits at intervals in the floor are left for baling purposes. Some trenches have to be built almost entirely of sand bags. Communication trenches almost invariably get full of water, and for the most part are not practicable the trenches are improved with a few loop holes at intervals for look out but men and snipers when not in use these are blinded. Loop holes and flaps are used as a certain extent but are difficult to conceal and afford a mark for the enemy.

The system of relief is 4 days in the front line and 4 days return bills to about [illegible] 4 miles rear off the front line. When in the front line the

— Sand bags
— Anchors ?
1, 2, 3 → Hurdles
4, 5 → Boards
6 → Fascines

WAR DIARY
or
INTELLIGENCE SUMMARY.
(Erase heading not required.)

Summary of Events and Information	Remarks and references to Appendices
...that actual front line trenches are refused every night, that a longer period causes the infantry to go up very depressing every effort is made to get the men fit and to if Baths and suffolks and if possible clean - washing to every some marches, fatigue work, classes of instruction etc etc are

have been no actual active operations. The fighting has being continuous, shelling of our trenches hardly a day passing without and artillery duels. As regards infantry there has been continued night and day and not as slow by day occasional knots of men to reconnoitre. Other than that else. casualties has been 18 killed and 16 wounded. | |

7th Inf.Bde.
3rd Div.

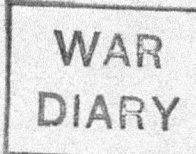

1st BATTN. THE WILTSHIRE REGIMENT.

F E B R U A R Y

1 9 1 5

WAR DIARY
or
INTELLIGENCE SUMMARY.

(Erase heading not required.)

Army Form C. 2118.

Hour, Date, Place	Summary of Events and Information	Remarks and references to Appendices
1st Feb LOCRE	A fairly quiet day, some shells fell near Sub Hd Qrs in men were wounded. Left the trenches there were no casualties. Relieved at 7.30 pm by 6th Fusiliers. 3 men wounded. 2nd Bn Gloster arrived strength of 19 officers joined Battalion	Bff
2nd Feb LOCRE	Rest	Bff b2
3rd Feb LOCRE	Rest	Bff
4th Feb LOCRE	Rest	Bff
5th Feb In huts near KEMMEL	Marched at 5.30 to the trenches and took over J section from 5th Fusiliers and H3 and H4 from Liverpool Scottish. Boy in firing line and I in support. 1 man killed and 2 wounded	Bff

Army Form C. 2118.

WAR DIARY
or
INTELLIGENCE SUMMARY.
(*Erase heading not required.*)

Instructions regarding War Diaries and Intelligence Summaries are contained in F.S. Regs., Part II. and the Staff Manual respectively. Title pages will be prepared in manuscript.

Hour, Date, Place	Summary of Events and Information	Remarks and references to Appendices
6th February In trenches near KEMMEL	A fairly quiet day in the trenches but a good deal of firing by night. Enemy shelled over KEMMEL	B.W
7th February In trenches near KEMMEL	A very quiet day. Nothing of note occurred 1 man wounded	B.W
8th February In trenches near KEMMEL	A very quiet day. Enemy shelled trenches slightly. Enemy dug out shrapnel at 3 p.m. 1 man killed.	B.W 62
9th February LOCRE	A very quiet day. Relieved by 5th Fusiliers and Liverpool Scottish at [?] relief complete by 10.30 pm. Returned to billets at LOCRE 1 man wounded. (East Kent)	B.W
10th February LOCRE	Rest. 2nd Lt Worthington attached strength 34 men Joined Battalion	B.W
11th February LOCRE	Rest. 2nd Lts Gorden (?) attached on probation " Peel } from H.A.C. " Scott " Baker-Cull	B.W

WAR DIARY
or
INTELLIGENCE SUMMARY.

(Erase heading not required.)

Army Form C. 2118.

	Summary of Events and Information	Remarks and references to Appendices
	Rest	O.C.
	Marched out from LOCRE at 5.30 p.m. To the Trenches and took over H3 & H4 from the LIVERPOOL SCOTTISH and the I Trench from No 5 & 2 FUSILIERS 1 coy in firing line 1 coy in support ~~on~~	O.C.
	A quiet day. ~~1 man killed~~ 1 wounded O.C.	O.C.
	A fairly quiet day. "K" Trench badly shelled, on our left. One shell over KEMMEL in the afternoon. One man ~~wounded~~ killed &	O.C.
	A fairly quiet day, KEMMEL HILL KEMMEL shelled, one man wounded. 2/Lt CROWDY joined battalion	O.C.

Army Form C. 2118.

WAR DIARY
or
INTELLIGENCE SUMMARY.
(Erase heading not required.)

Instructions regarding War Diaries and Intelligence Summaries are contained in F.S. Regs., Part II. and the Staff Manual respectively. Title pages will be prepared in manuscript.

Hour, Date, Place	Summary of Events and Information	Remarks and references to Appendices
17th February In Trenches near KEMMEL	A fairly quiet day. The 28th Div: lost some Trenches near ZWARTELEEN. The 9th Bde went to support them. We were not relieved in consequence. [all Trenches subsequently regained.] KEMMEL HILL shelled one man killed	JR.
18th February In Trenches near KEMMEL	A fairly quiet day. K Trenches slightly shelled 2 men wounded	JR.
19th February In Trenches near KEMMEL	A fairly quiet day. 9th Bde Transferred to 28th Div: 85th Bde Transferred to 3rd Div. The H.A.C. Transferred to 85th Bde. The allotment of Trenches altered. The R.I.R. Took over H3, H4, J1, and J10 from us. We took over K1 and support also S5 from the H.A.C. Rather heavy sniping 2 men killed, 1 man wounded.	JR.
20th February In Trenches near KEMMEL	A fairly quiet day. KEMMEL HILL shelled also the J Trenches. But no casualties occurred. Lt-Col Hoskil awarded the C.M.G, Capt Rowan the D.S.O Capt Hosley -- Military Cross, Capt Govedhart Continued on next sheet	JR.

Forms/C. 2118/10

WAR DIARY
or
INTELLIGENCE SUMMARY.
(Erase heading not required.)

Hour, Date, Place	Summary of Events and Information	Remarks and references to Appendices
20th Feby (cont)	2/Lt George mentioned in despatches. Pte Halton, Corpl Walker awarded D.C.M. Hon Cpt & Q'Mr Condon promoted Hon: Major. Coy S.M. Poolman, Sergt Meach, Sergt Wyatt, Corpl Russell mentioned in despatches. Two men wounded.	O/C
21st Feb in Trenches near KEMMEL	A fairly quiet day. KEMMEL shelled also slight shelling on our left. One man wounded one man missing.	O/C
22nd Feb 9th In Trenches LOCRE	A fairly quiet day. One German prisoner captured by C Coy near K.1. We were relieved by 85th Bde. The MIDDLESEX relieved us in J11 and Supports J2, J3 and R.E. SURREYS in K1 and supports and S5. Relief complete about 10.55 p.m. no casualties. The battalion returned to billets in LOCRE. SERGT HALES and Co/Sl OGILVIE promoted 2nd Lieutenants	O/C

Forms/C. 2118/10

WAR DIARY
or
INTELLIGENCE SUMMARY.
(Erase heading not required.)

	Summary of Events and Information	Remarks and references to Appendices
	Rest	J.C.
	Rest	J.C.
	Rest. 2Lt Upton, 2Lt Thorpe, 2Lt Morris joined the battalion.	J.C.
	Captain Harvey joined the battalion. marched to trenches at 6pm and relieved 85th Bde. 1 man killed.	RH 62
	Considerable shelling by enemy who searched the whole country round KEMMEL HILL Heavy rifle fire midnight. 1/2 killed one wounded	RH

Form/C. 2118/10

WAR DIARY
or
INTELLIGENCE SUMMARY.
(Erase heading not required.)

Instructions regarding War Diaries and Intelligence Summaries are contained in F.S. Regs., Part II. and the Staff Manual respectively. Title pages will be prepared in manuscript.

Hour, Date, Place	Summary of Events and Information	Remarks and references to Appendices
28th February In trenches near KEMMEL	Considerable shelling same as yesterday at 12 noon and 3 p.m. A good deal of rifle fire by night. 1 killed	AMcG Cas. for month K9. W19. M1 = 28
1st March In trenches near KEMMEL	Enemy dropped heavy shells at KEMMEL. Cross roads and trenches to the North a good many shells. 2 killed 2 wounded	BMcG
2nd March In trenches near KEMMEL	Enemy shelled Farm No. 1 LAITERIE also main road which runs past. Lieut. P.M.J. POWER. R.A.M.C. attd. 1st Welch killed. Buried at cemetery near CHATEAU KEMMEL. 2nd Lieut F.R. MUMFORD wounded. 1 killed 1 wounded.	BMcG
3rd March In trenches near KEMMEL	A quiet day. nothing of note occurred 2 wounded	BMcG BMcG

7th Inf.Bde.
3rd Div.

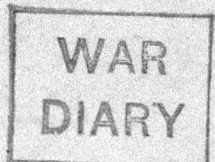

1st BATTN. THE WILTSHIRE REGIMENT.

M A R C H

1 9 1 5

WAR DIARY
or
INTELLIGENCE SUMMARY.
(Erase heading not required.)

Army Form C. 2118.

Hour, Date, Place	Summary of Events and Information	Remarks and references to Appendices
1st March In trenches near KEMMEL	Enemy dropped heavy shells at KEMMEL Cross roads and then traversed to the North. It good deal of rifle fire by night. 1 killed	
2nd March In trenches near KEMMEL	Enemy shelled farm Nr LA LAITERIE also Mansoord and J11 Otherwise quiet. Killed Lieut P.M.J. Power RAMC att'd 1st Wilts and one man. Buried in cemetery near CHATEAU KEMMEL. Wounded 2nd Lt F/K Mumford and one man.	
3rd March In trenches near KEMMEL	A quiet day. Nothing of note occurred. 2 wounded.	
4th March In trenches near KEMMEL LOCRE.	A quiet day. Relieved at 8pm by 3rd Middlesex. on I/K1 S5- J3 + J11 went in U2 J Royal Fusiliers. Returned to Billets at LOCRE.	

Army Form C. 2118.

WAR DIARY
or
INTELLIGENCE SUMMARY.
(Erase heading not required.)

Instructions regarding War Diaries and Intelligence Summaries are contained in F.S. Regs., Part II. and the Staff Manual respectively. Title pages will be prepared in manuscript.

Hour, Date, Place	Summary of Events and Information	Remarks and references to Appendices
5th March LOCRE	Rest	Batt
6th March LOCRE	Rest - Digging fatigue behind E trenches 7pm to 2am	Batt
7th March LOCRE	Rest	Batt
8th March LOCRE	Rest	Batt
9th March LOCRE	Rest	Batt
10th March LOCRE	Rest	Batt
11th March LOCRE	Rest	Batt
12th March LOCRE	Left Billets at LOCRE at 2.45am and marched via KEMMEL to the section of the trenches known as F in front of SPANBROEK MOLEN the battalion arrived in position at dawn about 5:30am and occupied four lines of trenches on the reverse side of the hill the	

WAR DIARY
or
INTELLIGENCE SUMMARY.
(Erase heading not required.)

Army Form C. 2118.

Hour, Date, Place	Summary of Events and Information	Remarks and references to Appendices
March 12th contd	Worcester regiment being in similar trenches on our right. The Battalion Headquarters were in the trench known as F2, about 50 yards in front of the front trench in which the Battalion was situated. These trenches were about 25 yards apart. The morning was dull and very misty so that the artillery bombardment which was to precede the assault on SPANBROEK MOLEN had to be delayed. The whole morning the remained misty and except for a certain amount of sniping and desultory gun fire was quiet. At 1 pm that mist began to clear and by 2.30 pm it was clear and the artillery bombardment began and continued with a slight pause till 4.10 pm, it consisted of field guns firing shrapnel to cut the north wire and large guns 74y of heavy high explosive to to beat down the parapets and blow in his trenches in this it appeared to be partly successful but it was afterwards observed that the enemy's front line trenches were almost intact. At 4.10 the infantry assault was launched by 2 coys of the 1st Wiltshires and 2 coys of the Worcesters. These regiment accompanied by a party of R.E.	DMy

WAR DIARY
or
INTELLIGENCE SUMMARY.
(Erase heading not required.)

Army Form C. 2118.

Summary of Events and Information	Remarks and references to Appendices

The remaining two companies being detailed as working parties. The front company (A Coy) made forward crossing the French known as F2 by means of flying bridges which had been placed in position almost early in the morning and leading through our lines by making the gaps which had been made specially the 34th Swiss. As soon as B & A company were clear of bridges as soon as B company followed them C and D (the working party) reconnaitring in the trenches of the bridge had for nearly the 2 hrs across to the bridge the enemy opened a very heavy rifle and machine gun fire on them, and only a few small isolated parties succeeded in getting up to the enemy's wire. B company (a distance of about 800 yds) and also came under a very heavy fire and were unable weft the remainder of A company to get more than 50 x from F2, at the same time most of the Worcestershire regiment on their right it appeared to be also unable to get on

WAR DIARY
or
INTELLIGENCE SUMMARY.
(Erase heading not required.)

Army Form C. 2118.

Hour, Date, Place	Summary of Events and Information	Remarks and references to Appendices
March 12th Cont'd	"B" Company endeavoured to march moved forward but their march to get very far and gradually before before starting about 1.30pm began to fall back onto F2 suffering considerably in doing so. Most of the remaining men of "B" Company who were in advance at "B" Company, of about 50 men of the Battalion under of darkness, it about 8pm the Battalion withdrew. It was observed that the enemy were holding this position very strongly and were not being unduly upset by our artillery fire, & the 2nd Leinster Regt were unable to support and the Royal Irish Rifles in reserve of KEMMEL that neither took an active part in the action. A company was commanded by Captain P.J.V. Vener-Johnson and Lieut Amours F2 was held by the East Surrey Regiment. The Battalion returned to Billets at LOCRE	[signature]

INTELLIGENCE SUMMARY.

(Erase heading not required.)

Place	Summary of Events and Information	Remarks and references to Appendices
	Casualties Capt P.J.V. Vaner Johnson ⎫ Killed Lieut O.J. Callely 2nd Lieut S.F. Hooper " D.G.H. Northcote (E. Buffs) Lieut C.C. Moore ⎫ Wounded 2nd Lieut A.H. Hales " S.M. Thayre Other Ranks 29 killed 12 missing 45 Wounded	15 off
	Rest 5 Pm heavy firing off on left towards ST ELOI 4th Bde stand strong reserve.	BN
	Standing by as strong reserve. March to trenches in front of KEMMEL and took over F2 F3 F6 & S2 from EAST SURREYS And H.A.C. 3 men wounded	Rgy

INTELLIGENCE SUMMARY.

(Erase heading not required.)

Instructions regarding War Diaries and Intelligence Summaries are contained in F. S. Regs., Part II. and the Staff Manual respectively. Title pages will be prepared in manuscript.

Hour, Date, Place	Summary of Events and Information	Remarks and references to Appendices
March 14th KEMMEL	A quiet day moved to trenches JII S9a S5 K#1 K1(8)	Bdy
March 18th KEMMEL	A quiet day nothing received occurred 2 men killed 3 wounded.	Bdy
March 19th KEMMEL	A quiet day. nothing received occurred	Bdy
March 20th KEMMEL	Quiet day not thing received occurred. 1 man wounded. Draft of 40 other ranks joined	Bdy
March 21st KEMMEL	A quiet day nothing received occurred 1 killed 1 wounded	Bdy
March 22nd KEMMEL	Enemy shelledered just north of LAITERIE 1 wounded rifle	Bdy
March 23rd LA CLYTE	Heavy burst of fire and shrapnel at 4.30am. talked about to enemy. No movement relieved by EAST SURREY norfolk by midnight. returned to billets at LA CLYTE 2 men wounded.	Bdy

INTELLIGENCE SUMMARY.

WAR DIARY
or
INTELLIGENCE SUMMARY.
(Erase heading not required.)

Instructions regarding War Diaries and Intelligence Summaries are contained in F.S. Regs., Part II. and the Staff Manual respectively. Title pages will be prepared in manuscript.

Hour, Date, Place	Summary of Events and Information	Remarks and references to Appendices
24th March LA CLYTE.	Rest	[sig]
25th March	Rest	[sig]
DICKEBUSH / LA CLYTE 26th March DICKEBUSH	Marched at 6.45 pm to DICKEBUSH went into Billets.	[sig]
27th March VORMEZEEL	Marched at 4 pm at took over trenche P(20) P(4b) P4(c) Q1 Q2 Q3 P6 South of St ELOI from H.A.C.	[sig]
28th March VORMEZEEL	A quiet day. 1 killed 1 wounded	[sig]
29th March DICKEBUSH	A quiet day. Relieved at 11pm by HAC	[sig]
30th March DICKEBUSH	Rest. Nothing doing and carrying parties	[sig]

Army Form C. 2118.

WAR DIARY
or
INTELLIGENCE SUMMARY.
(Erase heading not required.)

Instructions regarding War Diaries and Intelligence Summaries are contained in F.S. Regs., Part II. and the Staff Manual respectively. Title pages will be prepared in manuscript.

Hour, Date, Place	Summary of Events and Information	Remarks and references to Appendices
31st March VOORMEZEEL	Marched to trenches at 8.30pm and took over the same trenches from H.A.C.	BMy

B.M. Goodliffe
Captain
Adjutant 1st Bn. Wiltshire Regiment

7th Inf.Bde.
3rd Div.

WAR DIARY

1st BATTN. THE WILTSHIRE REGIMENT.

A P R I L

1 9 1 5

Army Form C. 2118.

WAR DIARY
or
INTELLIGENCE SUMMARY.
(Erase heading not required.)

Instructions regarding War Diaries and Intelligence Summaries are contained in F. S. Regs., Part II. and the Staff Manual respectively. Title pages will be prepared in manuscript.

Hour, Date, Place	Summary of Events and Information	Remarks and references to Appendices
1st April. VOORMEZEEL	A quiet day, a few shells over the village. All trenches are now in good condition.	[signature]
2nd April VOORMEZEEL	A quiet day. 3 men wounded	[signature]
3rd April VOORMEZEEL	A quiet day till 6pm when trench was bombarded with a very heavy trench mortar but no damage were done.	[signature]
4th April VOORMEZEEL DICKEBUSCHE	A quiet hot day. Relieved by Liverpool Scottish Battalion by about 11pm. Moved to billets at DICKEBUSCHE	[signature]
5th April DICKEBUSCHE	Rest.	[signature]
6th April DICKEBUSHE	Rest. O.C. Companies went to see new line. Captain R.H. BROOME wounded	[signature]
7th April DICKEBUSCHE	Rest.	[signature]

Army Form C. 2118.

WAR DIARY
or
INTELLIGENCE SUMMARY.
(Erase heading not required.)

Instructions regarding War Diaries and Intelligence Summaries are contained in F. S. Regs., Part II. and the Staff Manual respectively. Title pages will be prepared in manuscript.

Hour, Date, Place	Summary of Events and Information	Remarks and references to Appendices
8th April ELZENWALLE	March to the trenches at 7.15 pm and took over trenches known as P2 P2(a) P3 P4 P4(a) P4(b) P5, P6 and S7 from H.A.C. 2 companies in firing line the 1 in support 1 in reserve relief complete by 12.30 am 9th	RHy
9th April ELZENWALLE	A quiet day a good deal of rifle fire by night 1 man wounded	RHy
10th April ELZENWALLE	A quiet day some shrapnel over DICKEBUSCH lost 2 men wounded	RHy
11th April ELZENWALLE	A quiet a good deal of rifle fire by night 4 men wounded	RHy
12th April DICKEBUSCH	A quiet day Relieved by HAC by 11.30 pm A ZEPPELIN came over about 11.30 pm 3 men wounded	RHy

WAR DIARY
or
INTELLIGENCE SUMMARY.
(Erase heading not required.)

Instructions regarding War Diaries and Intelligence Summaries are contained in F.S. Regs., Part II. and the Staff Manual respectively. Title pages will be prepared in manuscript.

Hour, Date, Place	Summary of Events and Information	Remarks and references to Appendices
13th April DICKEBUSCH	Rest. Digging fatigue. 1 man wounded	R&g
14th April DICKEBUSCH	Rest. " " 1 " "	R&g
15th April DICKEBUSCH	Rest. "	R&g
16th April ELZENWALLE	Marched at 4.30 pm to Pretor and relieved H.A.C.	R&g
17th April ELZENWALLE	Very heavy gunfire to the left. The battalion demobilised with rapid fire at 4.30 pm as railway destroyed on left. One man wounded	R&g
18th April ELZENWALLE	6 pm heavy gun and rifle fire on left guest in Pretor. 30 large shells fell to the E of WICKEBUSCH CHATEAU	R&g
19th April ELZENWALLE	4 early guest-day. ELZENWALLE slightly shelled. Two men wounded.	R&g

WAR DIARY
or
INTELLIGENCE SUMMARY.
(Erase heading not required.)

Instructions regarding War Diaries and Intelligence Summaries are contained in F.S. Regs., Part II. and the Staff Manual respectively. Title pages will be prepared in manuscript.

Hour, Date, Place	Summary of Events and Information	Remarks and references to Appendices
20th April DICKEBUSCH	Rest. Digging fatigues	
21st April DICKEBUSCH	Rest. Digging fatigues	
22nd April DICKEBUSCH	Rest. Digging fatigues	
23rd April DICKEBUSCH	Heavy gun fire in the afternoon and evening to the North of YPRES Battalion stood by at ½ past an hours notice.	
24th April ELZENWALLE	Heavy gun fire North of YPRES still continuing by 2. Wallace HAC in Proctor of the Trenches commanding from DICKEBUSCH at Y.6.5. from Captain CARY-BARNARD took over command of the battalion vice Lt Col Harted sick	
25th April ELZENWALLE	Heavy gun fire North of YPRES a quiet day in our trenches but a good amount of shells by night 1 man killed 1 man wounded	

WAR DIARY
or
INTELLIGENCE SUMMARY.
(Erase heading not required.)

Army Form C. 2118.

Instructions regarding War Diaries and Intelligence Summaries are contained in F.S. Regs., Part II. and the Staff Manual respectively. Title pages will be prepared in manuscript.

Hour, Date, Place	Summary of Events and Information	Remarks and references to Appendices
26th April ELZENWALLE	Heavy gun fire to the cloth of YPRES. Quiet in our trenches. DICKEBUSCH shelled in afternoon. 2 men wounded.	
27th April ELZENWALLE	Heavy gun fire to the cloth of YPRES. Quiet in our trench. DICKEBUSCH shelled from East and North West. Transport moved back. 1 man wounded.	
28th April DICKEBUSCH	Relieved at 10 p.m. by H.A.C. marched back to billets at DICKEBUSCH. 2 men wounded. Gun fire North of YPRES continues	
29th April DICKEBUSCH	Rest	
30th April DICKEBUSCH	Rest	K.i.W. 1 +23

7th Inf.Bde.
3rd Div.

WAR
DIARY

1st BATTN. THE WILTSHIRE REGIMENT.

M A Y

1 9 1 5

WAR DIARY
or
INTELLIGENCE SUMMARY.
(Erase heading not required.)

Army Form C. 2118.

Hour, Date, Place	Summary of Events and Information	Remarks and references to Appendices
DICKEBUSCH 1st May	Rest	RAy
ELZENWALLE 2nd May	Shelled from DICKEBUSCH and road over P sector at the trenches behind relieving H.A.C. 3 men wounded	RAy
ELZENWALLE 3rd May	Quiet day to our front. Heavy fire from fire to the North. 1 man wounded	RAy
ELZENWALLE 4th May	Quiet day to our front. Enemy's guns active at night.	RAy
ELZENWALLE 5th May	Heavy gun fire to the North. Quiet during day to our front. Short bursts of rifle fire during night. 1 man killed	RAy
ELZENWALLE 6th May	Very quiet day 2nd Lieut WALTER ALFRED SCOTT killed	RAy

Army Form C. 2118.

WAR DIARY
or
INTELLIGENCE SUMMARY.
(Erase heading not required.)

Instructions regarding War Diaries and Intelligence Summaries are contained in F. S. Regs., Part II. and the Staff Manual respectively. Title pages will be prepared in manuscript.

Hour, Date, Place	Summary of Events and Information	Remarks and references to Appendices
ELZENWALLE. 7th May	A Quiet day. German aeroplane active over our lines. 1 wounded	[initials]
ELZENWALLE 8th May	Quiet day. 3 men wounded	[initials]
ELZENWALLE 9th May	Fairly quiet day. German aeroplane brought down by British just SE of ST. ELOI. 1 man killed 2 men wounded	[initials]
ELZENWALLE 10th May	Quiet day. considerable rifle fire to the left. 4 wounded	[initials]
ELZENWALLE 11th May	Relieved by HAC about 9 p.m. 1 killed, 1 wounded. Major BLAKE took over command of the Battalion from CAPT. CARY-BARNARD.	[initials]

(B 29 6) W 4141—463 100,000 9/14 H W V Forms/C. 2118/10

Army Form C. 2118.

WAR DIARY
or
INTELLIGENCE SUMMARY.
(Erase heading not required.)

Instructions regarding War Diaries and Intelligence Summaries are contained in F. S. Regs., Part II. and the Staff Manual respectively. Title pages will be prepared in manuscript.

Hour, Date, Place	Summary of Events and Information	Remarks and references to Appendices
12th May DICKEBUSHE	Rest	Bfy
13- May DICKEBUSCH	Rest	Bfy
14- May DICKEBUSCH	Rest	Bfy
15- May DICKEBUSCH	DICKEBUSCH shelled between 5 and 6 pm 1 man wounded	Bfy
16- May DICKEBUSCH	Rest	Bfy
17- May ELZENWALLE	Relieved H.A.C. in Poulton Battalion Headquarters the Moated to BRASSERIE, 9 Platoons in trenches 1 in reserve relief complete at midnight. 1 man wounded	Bfy
18- May ELZENWALLE	Very Quiet day	Bfy
19- May ELZENWALLE	Quiet day considerable sniping at night 2 men killed 1 wounded	Bfy

(9 29 6) W 4141—463 100,000 9/14 H W V Forms/C. 2118/10

Army Form C. 2118.

WAR DIARY
or
INTELLIGENCE SUMMARY.
(Erase heading not required.)

Instructions regarding War Diaries and Intelligence Summaries are contained in F.S. Regs., Part II. and the Staff Manual respectively. Title pages will be prepared in manuscript.

Hour, Date, Place	Summary of Events and Information	Remarks and references to Appendices
20th May ELZENWALLE	Enemy shelled over ELZENWALLE CHATEAU in the afternoon, considerable enfying by night. 1 man wounded	Bty
21st May ELZENWALLE	Relieved by H.A.C. Marched to billets in DICKEBUSCH. Two companies in RIDGEWOOD	Bty
22nd May DICKEBUSCH	Rest	Bty
23rd May DICKEBUSCH	Rest	Bty
24th May DICKEBUSCH	Rest	Bty
25th May ELZENWALLE	Left over Poperinghe from H.A.C. and O3 and O4 from B - A South Lancs. Relief complete by 11.30 pm. 2½ Coys in trenches ½ in Reserve	Bty

Forms/C. 2118/10

WAR DIARY or INTELLIGENCE SUMMARY.

(Erase heading not required.)

Hour, Date, Place	Summary of Events and Information	Remarks and references to Appendices
26. May	Quiet day. German aeroplanes rather active	Bty
27. May ELZENWALLE	Very quiet	Bty
28. May ELZENWALLE	Very quiet.	Bty / Bty
29. May	Quiet day. Germans active by night	Bty / Bty
30. May VICKEBUSCH	Quiet day. Relieved by HAC returned to billets at DICKEBUSCH	12 Bty
31. May DICKEBUSCH	Rest	1 Bty
		(w. batt. x+b. w. 19)

7th Inf.Bde.
3rd Div.

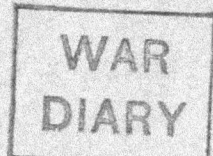

1st BATTN. THE WILTSHIRE REGIMENT.

J U N E

1 9 1 5

WAR DIARY
or
INTELLIGENCE SUMMARY.
(Erase heading not required.)

Army Form C. 2118.

Instructions regarding War Diaries and Intelligence Summaries are contained in F.S. Regs., Part II. and the Staff Manual respectively. Title pages will be prepared in manuscript.

Hour, Date, Place	Summary of Events and Information	Remarks and references to Appendices
June 1st DICKEBUSCH	Rest. 1 man wounded	Bty
June 2nd DICKEBUSCH	Rest	Bty
June 3rd VLAMERTINGHE	Heavy afternoon marched to a point S&W of VLAMERTINGHE and went into huts	Bty
June 4th HOOGE	Visited HOOGE defences in the evening and during night took over from LINCOLNS. The trenches were in a very bad state. 1 man wounded.	Bty
June 5th HOOGE	Fine hot, dry, quiet day. Large amount of work done and mainly conceded by engineers. C & D Coys went into reserve in ZOUAVE WOOD.	
June 6th HOOGE	Fine day. At 9.30 am the Germans opened a heavy attack W of HOOGE with all very heavy	

(9 29 6) W 4141—463 100,000 9/14 HWV Forms/C. 2118/10

Army Form C. 2118.

WAR DIARY
or
INTELLIGENCE SUMMARY.
(Erase heading not required.)

Instructions regarding War Diaries and Intelligence Summaries are contained in F. S. Regs, Part II. and the Staff Manual respectively. Title pages will be prepared in manuscript.

Hour, Date, Place	Summary of Events and Information	Remarks and references to Appendices
June 7th HOOGE	MINENWERFER and one medium one they fired about 21 rifle but were finally silenced 11.30am by our 9.2 Howitzer. 2 killed 20 withdrawn.	10.4
June 8th HOOGE	Hot & fine, a large quantity of tasked over was put out in front of the trenches. 2 killed 6 wounded.	11.4
June 9th YPRES	Fine and Thundery. Relieved by H.A.C. I killed 3 wounded. Returned to YPRES in the early morning and went into "Dug Outs" in the Ramparts to Rest.	12.4
June 11th Near YPRES	Marched to point one mile West of YPRES at 6.30pm	13.4

WAR DIARY
or
INTELLIGENCE SUMMARY.
(Erase heading not required.)

Army Form C. 2118.

Instructions regarding War Diaries and Intelligence Summaries are contained in F. S. Regs., Part II. and the Staff Manual respectively. Title pages will be prepared in manuscript.

Hour, Date, Place	Summary of Events and Information	Remarks and references to Appendices
June 11th YPRES	Rest	Asy
June 12th YPRES	Rest. Shewn list of men to proceed to hospital for exchange. Received a list of men found killed & 27 STANSFELD, SMITH and some men wounded 23 others.	Asy
June 13th YPRES	Rest	
June 14th YPRES	Rest	
June 15th	Marched to assembly trenches on MENIN Road west of HOOGE. Arrived in position about 11.45 p.m.	
June 16th 2.50 a.m.	Our Artillery commenced bombardment on German trenches situated between ROULERS Railway & a southern end of Y wood.	
4.15 a.m.	Artillery lengthened range and 9th Brigade assaulted first line of German trenches.	

WAR DIARY
or
INTELLIGENCE SUMMARY.
(Erase heading not required.)

Army Form C. 2118.

Hour, Date, Place	Summary of Events and Information	Remarks and references to Appendices
June 16th 4.20am	The 9th Brigade had carried the 1st line of German trenches. & 1 Platoon assaulted of C company assaulted trench at South end of Y wood which was taken without difficulty. A bombing party started to work up the Enemies trench in the direction of HOOGE, & made touch with Bonzus [?]. The remainder of C coy & D coy followed up. The leading men	
5am	reached a point some 100 yards from HOOGE village; meanwhile a communication trench was dug from CULVERT under MENIN road to Southern End of Y wood & Endeavour made to join up two pieces of German trench running East towards HOOGE until 6 am the situation remained unchanged.	
6 am	Some progress towards HOOGE was made - A point within 50 yards of the village being reached in the German trench. Between 6 am & 9 am the situation	BD

WAR DIARY or INTELLIGENCE SUMMARY.

Army Form C. 2118.

(Erase heading not required.)

Hour, Date, Place	Summary of Events and Information	Remarks and references to Appendices
June 16th	Remained unchanged. Rest of barricade & keeping the parapets was continued.	
9 am	The Germans advanced down two communication trenches from the North and under cover of a heavy fire started bombing heavily. We replied with grenades. This exchange lasted about 1½ hours.	
10.30	Our supply of grenades became exhausted and the Germans succeeded in driving in slowly the back down the trench. On retiring we suffered heavy casualties during this period of the action.	
11 am	We evacuated the Eastern portion of the German trench. We returned in the open & lost a considerable number of men in doing so. A counter attack was organised about this time to check the enemy's advance, but without success. As the officers & many men were shot down & the rear ranks made no progress.	[signature]

WAR DIARY
or
INTELLIGENCE SUMMARY.

(Erase heading not required.)

Army Form C. 2118.

Hour, Date, Place		Summary of Events and Information	Remarks and references to Appendices
June 16th	3 p.m.	Germans commenced a heavy bombardment of Y wood and the trenches which had been captured in the morning. Our guns replied by shelling the Germans about BELLEWARDE Lake presumably to break up any attempt at a counter attack. The situation remained unchanged in our trenches.	
	6.30 p.m.	Germans started a very heavy bombardment of Y wood which lasted about 1 hour.	
	8 p.m.	Germans fired a considerable number of gas shells in the neighbourhood of the MENIN road, but these only caused temporary inconvenience.	
	11 p.m.	SUFFOLKS started digging trench parallel to communication trench from corner of Y wood to culvert. The trench running Eastwards from the corner of Y wood was abandoned and blocked over a distance of 30 yds.	
June 17th	12.30 a.m.	Relieved by the SUFFOLKS	

WAR DIARY
or
INTELLIGENCE SUMMARY.
(Erase heading not required.)

Army Form C. 2118.

Hour, Date, Place	Summary of Events and Information	Remarks and references to Appendices
Jan 17th 1.30 am	The whole battalion had left & marched to billets between YPRES & VLAMERTINGE. Casualties during the action. Capt E.G. HARVEY killed 2nd Lieut A.B.P. McCLENAGHAN " Capt N.D. STEWART wounded 2nd Lieut F.S. GREGORY " " G.D. GORDON-HAKE " " C.S. GRAY " " R.J.A. PALMER " Capt A.E. STICKINGS wounded & prisoner 2/Lieut J.V.H. BARKER-MILLS wounded Other ranks killed 26 Missing believed killed 3 wounded 103 wounded & prisoners 3 missing 54 slightly wounded 6	

INTELLIGENCE SUMMARY.

(Erase heading not required.)

Hour, Date, Place	Summary of Events and Information	Remarks and references to Appendices
June 18	Battalion marched to HOOGE & took over trenches from D.W.	
June 19th	Fine. Trenches had been much damaged by shell fire. also seriously in elect in place.	
June 20	Germans shelled ZOUAVE wood from 6am to 7am & casualties.	
June 21	Desultory shelling throughout the day by enemy. Orders received from Brigade that an attack was to be made on redoubt "L" by 2 coys of Battalion. Fine & hot. A coy took up position in HOOGE trenches. 2 platoons in C1 and communication trench from tunnel to ISLAND POST. B coy in trenches north of ZOUAVE wood to support A coy.	
June 22	Bombardment took place 7.30am to 8pm at 8pm No 1 & 3 platoons attacked - but were held up by m. fire. The two officers leading attack	

INTELLIGENCE SUMMARY.

(Erase heading not required.)

Instructions regarding War Diaries and Intelligence Summaries are contained in F.S. Regs., Part II and the Staff Manual respectively. Title pages will be prepared in manuscript.

Hour, Date, Place	Summary of Events and Information	Remarks and references to Appendices
June 22	were shot & the men retired to own fire trenches. The action was broken off. The German parapets appeared to be but little damaged. Casualties 2/Lieut. A.M. McLEAN killed 2"" HEW BROADHURST wounded 2"" M.L. CARRINGTON —"— Other ranks 24. About midnight the Battalion were relieved & returned to billets near KLAMERTINGE.	
June 23	Rest	
June 24	Rest	
June 25	Rest	
June 26	An accident occurred in Camp in which the M.O. Lieut. PRYN was severely burnt. He subsequently died from the injuries received.	
June 27	Relieved 4 SOUTH LANCS in HOOGE Trenches	
June 28	C Coy relieves North Irish Horse & CYCLISTS in trenches west of HOOGE.	

INTELLIGENCE SUMMARY.

(Erase heading not required.)

Instructions regarding War Diaries and Intelligence Summaries are contained in F.S. Regs., Part II. and the Staff Manual respectively. Title pages will be prepared in manuscript.

Hour, Date, Place	Summary of Events and Information	Remarks and references to Appendices
June 28	Dull. Enemy's trench mortars put several shells into trenches about BULL FARM in Evening.	
June 29	Showery & warm. B Coy shelled with trench mortars. Casualties 2 killed 8 wounded. A Coy relieve B Coy in HOOGE Trenches	
30	Enemy shelled MENIN Road & broke in our trenches in several places. A large amount of work was done on trenches & to strengthen fortification of HOOGE.	

for Capt Gouchart.

P.T. Reed 2/Lt
1st Wilts.

7th Inf.Bde.
3rd Div.

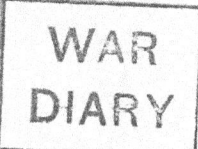

1st BATTN. THE WILTSHIRE REGIMENT.

J U L Y

1 9 1 5

Army Form C. 2118.

WAR DIARY
INTELLIGENCE SUMMARY. 1st Wiltshire Regt.
(Erase heading not required.)

Instructions regarding War Diaries and Intelligence Summaries are contained in F.S. Regs., Part II. and the Staff Manual respectively. Title pages will be prepared in manuscript.

Hour, Date, Place	Summary of Events and Information	Remarks and references to Appendices
1st July 1915 HOOGE	Quiet throughout day until evening when a heavy bombardment took place against ZOUAVE WOOD & communication trenches. - No casualties. Battalion relieved by R.I.R. relief completed 12.30 a.m. —	MMB
2nd July BUSSEBOOM	Resting & cleaning up. Sunny fine	MMB
3rd " — —	Usual parades, bomb instruction; several excuses. Sunny fine	MMB
4th " — —	Usual parade, church service at 7 p.m. Sunny fine	MMB
5th " HOOGE	Relieved R.I.R. in trenches, relief completed 12.20 a.m. Two men wounded. Dull fine	MMB
6th " — —	Dull showery; wire was placed during night in front of C3 r.c. Two wounded. —	MMB
7th " — —	Bright morning dull showery, visited by General Gendesome & Staff - three men wounded. —	MMB
8th " — —	Bright sunny; relieved by R.I.R. relief completed 12.30 a.m. / man killed. Veillul —	MMB

Army Form C. 2118.

WAR DIARY
or
INTELLIGENCE SUMMARY.
(Erase heading not required.)

Instructions regarding War Diaries and Intelligence Summaries are contained in F.S. Regs., Part II. and the Staff Manual respectively. Title pages will be prepared in manuscript.

Hour, Date, Place		Summary of Events and Information	Remarks and references to Appendices
July 9th	BUSSEBOOM	Bivouac near Reninghome. Bright fine day. Cleaning up & resting	MOS
10th	"	Usual parades	MOS
11th	"	Church service at 11 a.m. Moved to bivouac near ABEELE in afternoon.	MOS
12th	ABEELE	Settling & improving camp	MOS
13th	"	Fine & dull. Usual parades.	MOS
14th	"	Usual parade, heavy rain in evening. Bivouacs made of waterproof sheets, keep out rain well.	MOS
15th	"	Wet & cold, usual parades.	MOS
16th	"	Heavy rain in evening clearing night. Usual parades	MOS
17th	"	Bright sunny day. Usual parades. Church Parade 11.45 a.m.	MOS
18th	"	Bright day. Usual parades. Church parade 11.45 a.m.	MOS

WAR DIARY or INTELLIGENCE SUMMARY.

(Erase heading not required.)

Army Form C. 2118.

Instructions regarding War Diaries and Intelligence Summaries are contained in F. S. Regs., Part II and the Staff Manual respectively. Title pages will be prepared in manuscript.

Hour, Date, Place		Summary of Events and Information	Remarks and references to Appendices
July			
19th	ABEELE	Usual parade, bright day.	
20th	"	Visited new trench line at ST. ELOI.	
21st	ST. ELOI	Relieved K.O.Y.L.I. at St Eloi relief completed 12.15 a.m. 1 man killed, 2 wounded. — Lt. Colonel W.S. Brown joined at transport	
22nd	"	Showery, quiet in trenches, no casualties. —	
23rd	"	Showery. A mine was exploded by us near Crater. Lt. Colonel Brown arrived in trenches & took over command from Temporary Lt. Colonel (Temp) Blake D.S.O. —	
24th	"	Fine hot day, very quiet, relieved by 2nd S. Lancs relief completed 1.30 p.m.	
25th	DICKEBUSCH HUTS	Hot & fine voluntary church service in morning Cleaning up & refitting. —	
26th	"	Usual parade. Hot & showery. —	
27th	"	Visited T. Trenches preparatory to occupation. Hot & fine usual parade. —	
28th	ST. ELOI.	Relieved Worcester Regt. in T. Trenches one other wounded	

Army Form C. 2118.

WAR DIARY
or
INTELLIGENCE SUMMARY.
(Erase heading not required.)

Instructions regarding War Diaries and Intelligence Summaries are contained in F.S. Regs., Part II and the Staff Manual respectively. Title pages will be prepared in manuscript.

Hour, Date, Place	Summary of Events and Information	Remarks and references to Appendices
July 29th ST. ELOI.	German mine exploded 7 p.m. 10 yards in front of trenches. 1 man wounded.	mms
30th " — " —	Rainy. German mine exploded. Casualties 1 killed	mms
31st " — " —	Fine. quiet day. one man wounded	mms

N. Brown Lt. Colonel
O/C, 1st Yorkshire Regt

14/8/15

7th Inf.Bde.
3rd Div.

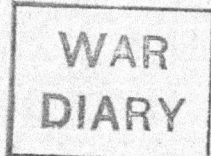

1st BATTN. THE WILTSHIRE REGIMENT.

A U G U S T

1 9 1 5

WAR DIARY
or
INTELLIGENCE SUMMARY. 1st Wiltshire Regt.

(Erase heading not required.)

Army Form C. 2118.

Hour, Date, Place	Summary of Events and Information	Remarks and references to Appendices
1st August 1915. ST. ELOI.	Mine exploded 15 yards in front of our trenches at 7.15 p.m. one man killed, 12 wounded (B Coy.)	mss
2nd —"— —"—	Relieved by 7th Yorkshire Regt (2nd new army) relief completed 2.45 a.m. — Casualties 6 wounded. —	mss
3rd —"— ST. JEAN	Bivouacked during day, & at night took over new line near ST. JEAN from 2nd Leinsters, relief completed 1.45 a.m. no casualties. — Very cool, heavy showers in evening. —	mss
4th —"— —"—	Showery. Spasmodic shelling along front & support trenches, one man wounded. —	mss
5th —"— —"—	Fair shot, fairly quiet along front.	mss
6th —"— —"—	Quiet along front. Fine day —	mss
7th —"— —"—	Occasional shelling, two men killed and two wounded.	mss
8th —"— —"—	Spasmodic shelling. Weather fine. Casualties	mss
9th —"— —"—	9th one killed, 1st one killed, not yet wounded. —	mss

Army Form C. 2118.

WAR DIARY
or
INTELLIGENCE SUMMARY.
(Erase heading not required.)

Instructions regarding War Diaries and Intelligence Summaries are contained in F. S. Regs., Part II. and the Staff Manual respectively. Title pages will be prepared in manuscript.

Hour, Date, Place		Summary of Events and Information	Remarks and references to Appendices
10th August	ST. JEAN.	Quiet on front. Sniper shot one man wounded, one man killed.	mps
11th	— " —	Main C.T. trench shelled by whiz bangs.	
		Relieved by R.I.R. relief completed 12 m.n. — moved to dugouts in Canal bank 1½ miles back. One man wounded. —	mps
12th	— " — Canal Bank	Battalion rested, cleaned & refitted after 14 days in trenches. — Copper shop started on	
13th	— " — "	13th Coy dugouts. —	
14th	— " — "	Company officers visited trenches at Cross Roads farm for 14th. — Parados impossible owing to hostile air craft frequently flying over.	
15th	— " — LA BRIQUE	Relieved 6th Worcesters in trenches, relief completed 12.15 a.m. Casualties Sergt Harris C. Coy killed on road during relief. rapid file having been opened suddenly by enemy.	mps
		Fine night. —	
16th	— " — "	Worked hard cleaning & clearing trenches. Showery in morning. Other fine. —	
		Brigadier visited trenches —	
17th	— " — "	Quiet day. Bright sun, a little whizz banging Casualties 1 wounded D Coy.	

(9 29 6) W 4141—463 100,000 9/14 H W V Forms/C. 2118/10

Army Form C. 2118.

WAR DIARY or INTELLIGENCE SUMMARY.

(Erase heading not required.)

Hour, Date, Place	Summary of Events and Information	Remarks and references to Appendices
18th August LA BRIQUE	Artillery rather active, also enemy's aeroplanes. Hot in morning esp. Fine day. Info that Maddens shot had a special patrol for which night, met no Germans, but located a new trench.	MSS
19th " "	Artillery active. Fine day. Relieved by 1st Leicestershire Regt. Relief completed 1 a.m. — Lost Coy arrived at bivouac 4 a.m. — 23rd. — Casualties 1 man wounded.	MSS
20th " OUDERDOM	Bivouacs at Ouderdom; cleaning up, refitting 2 company parades. — Coys slept in red Fine in 20th showing in 21st. — Party of 250 were employed digging in ZILLEBEKE from 8pm to 3am. 2 Casualties. 22nd Fine	MSS
21st " "		Bivac
22nd " "	Resting — Battalion was on chety. Fine S.M. HADDRIL was presented with DCM by Gen. HALDANE.	Bir
23rd " "	Resting. Fine. Battalion marched to HOOGE & relieved 1st N. STAFFORDS. Relief complete to 10.40pm	Bir
24 " "		
25 HOOGE	Fine. Enemy shelled our S.Phots. Own heavies replied vigorously — own bombard was most effective & stopped the enemy artillery fire. 14 casualties C Coy reached "Gate" in HOOGE.	Bir

Forms/C. 2118/10

WAR DIARY or INTELLIGENCE SUMMARY

Army Form C. 2118.

(Erase heading not required.)

Hour, Date, Place	Summary of Events and Information	Remarks and references to Appendices
26th August HOOGE	Quiet day: Corps Commander visited trenches with Gen: HALDANE. Worked hard at HOOGE defences and clearing trenches which were in a very foul condition after recent fighting. Attempted to line front of 919 but the party were seen by the enemy & had one 3 casualties.	
27th " " "	B Coy relieved C Coy in MINE CRATER. Orders were received to occupy & fortify an advanced trench running in front of STABLES & connect it with 2nd S. LANCS, who had to dig up to the Stables. D Coy were detailed for this operation. A Bombing party occupied this trench after dark & the working party commenced digging having received the Stables. A very heavy bombing duel ensued, our grenadiers throwing some 500 bombs at the advanced German trench. Bombing activities hindered work on defences but the trench was occupied	

Army Form C. 2118.

WAR DIARY
or
INTELLIGENCE SUMMARY.
(Erase heading not required.)

Instructions regarding War Diaries and Intelligence Summaries are contained in F. S. Regs., Part II. and the Staff Manual respectively. Title pages will be prepared in manuscript.

Hour, Date, Place	Summary of Events and Information	Remarks and references to Appendices
27th August HOOGE (cont.)	Up to the stables & handed to relieving but R.I.R. who placed a small garrison in it. The Battalion was relieved by R.I.R. and returned to Zivonaes N/W of DICKEBUSH. Casualties 1 killed 7 wounded.	
28th — / N.W. DICKEBUSCHE Bivouac	Resting. Fine	
29th — " — " —	Resting. Voluntary Church parade with Band mid afternoon. Corps marched to POPERINGHE to bathe.	
30th — " — " —	Rain most of the day. Battalion marched to HOOGE in the evening and relieved R.I.R. B Coy garrisoned Crate trenches. Relief completed 1.30 a.m. Casualties 1 killed 1 wounded	
31st — " — HOOGE.	Quiet day. Work was done in the advanced trench towards the stables & in 1st retrenchment. At one point the fire on trenches Ten very close to ours; parties of the enemy were observed hutting	

Forms/C. 2118/10

INTELLIGENCE SUMMARY.

(Erase heading not required.)

Hour, Date, Place	Summary of Events and Information	Remarks and references to Appendices
Aug 31st HOOGE	Out barbed wire. Some was laid in an trench by the German, who approached within 27 yards of our advanced post. They apparently were not aware that we held it. Action had been given not to fire and attract attention, as we were working parties were digging in very exposed places. Casualties 1 wounded.	

NPBrown Lt.-Colonel
Comdg. 1st. Bn. Wiltshire Regt.

7th Inf.Bde.
3rd Div.

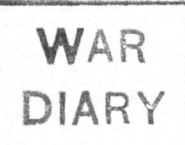

1st BATTN. THE WILTSHIRE REGIMENT.

S E P T E M B E R

1 9 1 5

WAR DIARY
or
INTELLIGENCE SUMMARY.
(Erase heading not required.)

Army Form C. 2118.

Instructions regarding War Diaries and Intelligence Summaries are contained in F.S. Regs., Part II. and the Staff Manual respectively. Title pages will be prepared in manuscript.

Hour, Date, Place	Summary of Events and Information	Remarks and references to Appendices
September 1st HOOGE	Our heavy artillery bombarded German lines from daylight to 4.30 a.m. Enemy retaliated by shelling heavily Zouave & Sanctuary Woods. Trenches were very much damaged. All Telephone wires to front trenches were cut. Communication between two platoons in in places, & sulphate shells. Casualties 4 killed 26 wounded and Capt C.D.V. CARY-BARNARD D.S.O wounded 2ⁿᵈ Lieut. R.W.N. JEANS —"— " " C.A. PREST —"— " " R.W. BIRD —"—	BN
Sept 2ⁿᵈ HOOGE	Our artillery bombarded German lines from 3.55 a.m. Enemy retaliated immediately & kept up an intermittent fire throughout the day. Our trenches were blown in in one or two places. Enemy's fire in excess of in the explosion & the Respect was asked to for retaliation, this was answered	BN

WAR DIARY
or
INTELLIGENCE SUMMARY.
(Erase heading not required.)

Army Form C. 2118.

Instructions regarding War Diaries and Intelligence Summaries are contained in F.S. Regs., Part II. and the Staff Manual respectively. Title pages will be prepared in manuscript.

Hour, Date, Place	Summary of Events and Information	Remarks and references to Appendices
Sept 2nd HOOGE	by the Corps; At about 3 A.M. an artillery opened a very heavy fire on the German lines. The enemy evidently expected an attack & concentrated an intense fire on our & front trenches. The C.T.s were swept with shrapnel & in many places blown in by heavy shells. All lines were cut. C Coy were occupying Cable Trenches, A Coy the left sector with 2 platoons in support. Two two platoons were moved up to reinforce the firing line; & two platoons from B Coy were pushed up into A.G. This deployment was carried out without casualties; The men were moved at communication trenches in small parties. Dugouts in the Cable were wrecked & heavy casualties sustained here. The fire trench on the left were obliterated & the main C.T. completely blown in in many	These 2 platoons were moved up by 2nd & 2ᵈ machine with great skill, under a heavy bombardment & suffered no casualties — 2ⁿᵈ Lt Snelgar was in command of A Coy — 1915 Eliot

WAR DIARY or INTELLIGENCE SUMMARY

Hour, Date, Place	Summary of Events and Information	Remarks and references to Appendices
Sept 2nd HOOGE	At dark B Coy relieved C Coy & D Coy was sent up to work at repairing the firing line. Heavy rain all night. Very little rifle fire. Casualties 2/LIEUT C.B. PREST wounded at 1.25 Other ranks 14 killed / 38 wounded / 2 missing believed killed.	
Sept 3rd — " —	Heavy rain all day. Enemy's infantry very quiet. Following message received from GEN. HALDANE — "Convey to WILTSHIRE regiment my appreciation of stout-hearted manner they stood bombardment yesterday. Regret heavy casualties." An artillery duel. Enemy's trenches in the early morning. Rep replied to from a on fire trenches. subhats & communication trenches Relieved by R.I.R. relief complete 1 A.M. Batt. returned to ramparts at YPRES. Casualties 3 wounded	

WAR DIARY or INTELLIGENCE SUMMARY.

(Erase heading not required.)

Hour, Date, Place	Summary of Events and Information	Remarks and references to Appendices
Sept 4th YPRES.	The Bn. rested in Ramparts at Ypres; rain most of day; shells coming over, no casualties.	mss
Sept 5th "	Resting in rampart. The C.O. spoke to the Companies & said that the B.G.C. was very pleased with their recent work. N.C.O's & men who had been selected by the Offr Cos Coys were congratulated on their work. A heavy bombardment all morn, men compared to dug outs. Major Warlake D.S.O received orders to take over command of the 2nd Bn. West Yorkshire Regt. with the temporary rank of Lt. Colonel.	EoP
Sept 6th YPRES.	Resting in ramparts. Intermittent shelling by Enemy. Most of the day. Re cross Battalion diggers opt dusk at HOOGE & SANCTUARY WOOD. (2 casualties) Fine.	EoP
Sept 7th YPRES.	" Re cross Battalion diggers opt dusk at HOOGE & SANCTUARY WOOD	EoP
Sept 8th "	" at HOOGE & SANCTUARY WOOD	EoP
Sept 9th "	" Bn. relieves R.I.R. in HOOGE Trenches. Relief complete 12.30 a.m.	EoP

WAR DIARY or INTELLIGENCE SUMMARY.

(Erase heading not required.)

Instructions regarding War Diaries and Intelligence Summaries are contained in F.S. Regs., Part II. and the Staff Manual respectively. Title pages will be prepared in manuscript.

Hour, Date, Place	Summary of Events and Information	Remarks and references to Appendices
Sept 10th HOOGE	Fine. Quiet day. 1 Casualty. D Coy in Crater.	EOR
Sept 11th HOOGE	Fine. Our artillery shelled enemy trenches & craters. In the afternoon enemy replied by shelling crater & left sector. 2 casualties.	EOR
Sept 12th HOOGE	Fine. Our artillery shelled enemy trenches &c. Afternoon quiet. Battalion relieved in evening by R.I.R. 2nd S.L.M.R.S. Mackail. Went to rest camp Resting. Fine.	EOR EOR
Sept 13th BUSSEBOOM	" "	EOR
" 14th " "		EOR
" 15th " "	Battalion inspected by Gen Plumer II R. Coy Army	EOR
" 16th " "	100 men worked on HOOGE at night. Regimental sports	EOR
" 17th " "	Party of 200 men worked at HOOGE at night.	EOR EOR
	Major C.V. CORY - BARNARD D.S.O. Left to take up Staff Captain with 51 Brigade. Arr. HOOGE Regt Concert in the Evening.	EOR

INTELLIGENCE SUMMARY.

(Erase heading not required.)

Instructions regarding War Diaries and Intelligence Summaries are contained in F.S. Regs., Part II and the Staff Manual respectively. Title pages will be prepared in manuscript.

Hour, Date, Place	Summary of Events and Information	Remarks and references to Appendices
Sept 18 - BUSSEBOOM	Resting - Following message received from 2nd Army. D.C. Medals have been awarded to No 7788 Sergt A. BELL and No 8135 Sergt F. LEACH 1st W Yorks and Please convey Army Commanders Congratulations to recipients. Battalion marched to YPRES at 6.30pm + billetted in the ramparts. 200 men were out digging during the night	EP
September 19. YPRES.	Constant shelling throughout the day. Our artillery bombarded HOOGE positions. Enemy replied - a large number of shells fell in the Town + on ramparts. Casualties 3 wounded. At night the whole Battalion were out digging + carrying until early morning.	EP
— 20 YPRES.	Shelling on both sides continued. Early morning bombardment of enemies position at HOOGE	

WAR DIARY or INTELLIGENCE SUMMARY.

(Erase heading not required.)

Hour, Date, Place	Summary of Events and Information	Remarks and references to Appendices
September 20 YPRES	Active rehearsals by enemy on town & ramparts. Battalion out digging all night. Casualties 2 wounded	
21 YPRES	Heavy bombardment during the day. Town & ramparts shelled by enemy. The whole Battalion was out digging at night. Casualties 3 wounded.	
22 YPRES	Enemy replied to our bombardment of HOOGE positions by shelling town ramparts. Continuous firing throughout the day. Very heavy shells were put into YPRES in the morning, probably 15 inch. Ramparts damaged, 1 culvert cracked. The whole Battalion was out digging at night until early morning.	
23 YPRES	As on previous day. Heavy shelling of both sides. The men had been able to get very little	

WAR DIARY or INTELLIGENCE SUMMARY.

Army Form C. 2118.

(Erase heading not required.)

Hour, Date, Place	Summary of Events and Information	Remarks and references to Appendices
September 23 YPRES	Slept - Being out all night & during the day the noise & constant moving out of cellars & dug outs to culverts & trenches was very disturbing. All ranks were obviously feeling the strain & lack of sleep. The whole Battalion was again out all night digging & carrying. Casualties killed 4 wounded 13 - been the during the past 5 days had been firm.	EoP
September 24 YPRES	Firm. Orders for operations on 25th received. The Battalion was to be in close support to R I R & 2 S.LANCS who were assaulting Enemies trenches at HOOGE in front of BELLEWARDE Lake. Report covering these operations Positions were taken up on the night of 24/25 as follows -	EoP

WAR DIARY or INTELLIGENCE SUMMARY.

(Erase heading not required.)

Army Form C. 2118.

Hour, Date, Place	Summary of Events and Information	Remarks and references to Appendices
Sept 24/25th HOOGE	B Coy two sects S.E. of old assembly trenches S. of MENIN ROAD. A Coy 2 platoons H.12, 2 platoons new tank dug outs to rear of H.12. D Coy R.S.5. C Coy 2 platoons R.S.4, 2 platoons HALFWAY HOUSE. C & D Coys were carrying until 1.30am. Battalion was in position by 2am. Battalion dressing station & Bn HQ was completed close to R.S.5. The Bombardment commenced at 3.50am the enemy replied within 30 seconds by fierce artillery fire a few feet in front of H.12, chiefly with field guns & small howrs. A curtain of shrapnel was put in front of H.12 & the assembly trenches there which was main (ruined for 2 hrs. The MENIN ROAD was swept with shrapnel, as were the main c.ts. Griffin Union & Earth Streets. H.12 shrapnel was hot over H.12 (A Coy) & the sets S of MENIN ROAD (B Coy). Telephone wires to all trenches & Bn HQ were immediately cut. The trenches occupied by B & A did not suffer much from heavy shell fire except S.S.D. The left of R.S.5 (D Coy) which was badly blown in at junctions of c.ts. Certain other hits	

INTELLIGENCE SUMMARY.

(Erase heading not required.)

Hour, Date, Place	Summary of Events and Information	Remarks and references to Appendices
September 25th HOOGE	were obviously marked & a constant fire of shrapnel was kept up on these places throughout the day. The main C.T.s were flooded in many places but were not rendered unserviceable. During the operations they were of the utmost value for evacuating the wounded & relieving congestion in the front lines. At 7.30 a.m. an order known as "1 coy to the first line" was received from Bde Hq. This was carried out by "B" coy who occupied a portion of "C" coy trench, A coy R.I.R. on their left and a small part of 2nd S. Lancs on the right. Late in the day the front line was stretching to be too crowded & 1 platoon of the coy was withdrawn to C.T.s N. of MENIN road. 3 coys of the batn were in position in the firing line to support the attack & 1 in reserve.	

INTELLIGENCE SUMMARY.

(Erase heading not required.)

Hour, Date, Place	Summary of Events and Information	Remarks and references to Appendices
Sept 25th HOOGE	Re our right hand guns was put out of action & the emplacements destroyed by shell fire. Re disposition of the Battalion after B Coy had moved up remained unchanged during the day. Heavy shelling continued during the day. C & C5 suffered severely, also C3s from GATE to FIRE TRENCH, there was trouble in places every little cover against shrapnel remained in the right sector. No definite information was received as the result of the attack, it was believed that 2 coys of the RIR had gone forward, to our right. A few trenches was occupied by B coy which was known as RIR HQs in front & No Communication was established with the coys who had gone forward. The situation was very uncertain. Our troops on the left were	

INTELLIGENCE SUMMARY.

(Erase heading not required.)

Hour, Date, Place	Summary of Events and Information	Remarks and references to Appendices
Sept 25th HOOGE	Ordered to relieve from the Enemies trenches which had apparently been Captured, not even until 6 a Sept that this fact leaked to Bde Capitaine him in doubt so. Orders were received at 7.30 to for the Bn to relieve the R.I.R. & 2 S. Lancs who had been beat together origined time. Two Coys of the Bn. were eventually moved up into the front line with 2 more of the 4th S. Lancs together than but out of action. B Coy were relieved & sent back to days a.b at HALFWAY HOUSE. D & C Coys garrisoned the firing line with A in Support. [scratched out lines]	[illegible]

INTELLIGENCE SUMMARY

(Erase heading not required.)

Hour, Date, Place	Summary of Events and Information	Remarks and references to Appendices

Sept 25
HOOGE
	Relief of R.I.R. & 2nd Scots Gds. Completed at about 1.30 a.m. The enemy continued to shell the C.T.'s & approaches to front at intervals until 2 a.m.
	The front trenches especially on the right were found to be in a very demolished condition, the line in front practically destroyed. A many dead were lying about; a large number of bombs were buried & others rendered unserviceable.
	The Batn at the end of the day consisted of 400 rifles, the majority of whom were in a very exhausted condition, then had been very few opportunities of pillage any sleep during the past week.
	Casualties Officers 2/Lt Emanuel killed
	            Capt. R.H. Upton wounded
	Other ranks killed 15
	                wounded 53
		Officers present with Bn.
		H.Q. Lt Col W.S. Brown
		   Lt. Colonel W.S. Brown
		   2nd Lt. Q. adjt. E.F. Paul
		   Lieut & Mediston R.A.M.C.
		
		A.Coy. Capt. S. Ogilvie
		   2nd Lt. Borden
		   " J.T. Snedgen
		   " F.E. Pettit.
		           — HALES
		B.Coy. Captain Hill
		   2nd Lt. HILL
		          (machine gun)
		   2nd Lt. Greece
		   " Maybrook
		   " Emanuel
		
		C.Coy. Capt. R. Kennedy
		   2/Lt. so Russell
		   2/Lt. Cartwright
		
		D.Coy. Capt. A.H. Upton
		   Lieut H. Millar
		   2/Lt. Terry

Hour, Date, Place	Summary of Events and Information	Remarks and references to Appendices
Operations Sept 25th	Points of Interest: 1. Value of assembly of 6/6 new trench dug overnight. B Coy suffered only few casualties in shift s of MENIN road. These trenches had apparently got been registered upon but under observation. Part of D Coy had any 1 casualty in the new front line in shaving the night to the rear of the trench on the M.R. The new trench was carefully concealed with turf whilst local cover was constructed to afford protection from shrapnel + falling pieces of shell. This trench was never observed. 2. Telephonic Communication was of no value. Runners seem the essential to establish some simple form of evidence.	Bro

INTELLIGENCE SUMMARY.

(Erase heading not required.)

Hour, Date, Place	Summary of Events and Information	Remarks and references to Appendices

Signalling between fore trenches & rear not satisfactory.

3. The junction of C.T.s were registered points known shelled during the day. This is not the most suitable place to post guards to direct movement to + up & down the trenches. Head Cover should be erected for such posts. The majority of C.T. barrel greenhouses killed.

4. The C.T.s front flares is a main feature were most employed the day time of the utmost value for warning unarmed & relieving carriers at the past times.

5. The initiative of all ranks in many portion of Batt. H.Q. must delay a hostilely many casualties were occasioned & by activities from sniper weapons to the enemy

INTELLIGENCE SUMMARY.

(Erase heading not required.)

Hour, Date, Place	Summary of Events and Information	Remarks and references to Appendices

Headquarters.

6. We did not attack the main advanced position in having a dressing station so advanced & exposed hostile. Only walking cases could be dealt with almost the day & sort could well have been attended to from the back.

7. Artillery 5.6" off 7th OT's were of value in observing & distributing the enemies fire. A large amount of ammunition was expended on the 5.6" off Costre St in front of F2. Rear was unoccupied. Dummy trenches & barricades on the road might have been of considerable value in drawing the enemies fire from our had trenches, if time had been available to construct them.) BP

INTELLIGENCE SUMMARY.

(Erase heading not required.)

Hour, Date, Place	Summary of Events and Information	Remarks and references to Appendices
Sept 26th HOOGE.	Fine. Both occupied clearing ground when possible. The trenches have very wet; a great amount of labour required to render them the position in a satisfactory state. Telephone communication was restored by 4th Royal Fusiliers. During the relief bombing activities from Loke out in immediate right followed by rifle & m.g. fire along the front. Artillery support was called for & the Enemy Gallery promptly opened fire on the HOOGE front. The Enemy replied by shelling our fire trenches. The trenches were greatly congested at the time owing to the relief. D Coy suffering several casualties. Relief was suspended for a time and	

INTELLIGENCE SUMMARY

(Erase heading not required.)

Instructions regarding War Diaries and Intelligence Summaries are contained in F.S. Regs., Part II and the Staff Manual respectively. Title pages will be prepared in manuscript.

Hour, Date, Place	Summary of Events and Information	Remarks and references to Appendices
Sept 27th Bivouac BUSSEBOOM	5th Corps. No further action developed between with 5th Div was eventually carried out. The bn marched back to billets Bivouac at BUSSEBOOM arriving at 5 a.m. 27th — Casualties 2 killed 22 wounded (Sergt Sainsbury was killed) Resting — heavy rain during the day	
Sept 28th — // —	Cloudy, cold, rain at night & during the day. The bn were not able to make use of baths at POPERINGHE Much parade time.	
Sept 29th — // —		
Sept 30th — // —	Orders received from Bde at 7 am to move at 2 hrs notice. HQ c had already moved & WORCESTERS were ready to go.	

INTELLIGENCE SUMMARY.

(Erase heading not required.)

Hour, Date, Place	Summary of Events and Information	Remarks and references to Appendices
Sept 30th	Orders received at 1.15pm for Batt. to move as soon as possible to KRUISSTRAAT where it came under orders of 8th Brigade. By 5pm the whole Batn was billeted at KRUISSTRAAT. During the night 125 men were employed carrying Bombs to 8th Bde HQ in MAPLE COPSE. No further orders were received during the night, the Batn remained in reserve during the operations. Fighting strength of Bn reduced to 450.	Enc. W.P. Brown Lt. Colonel O/C 12th Middx. Regt

7th Inf.Bde.
3rd Div.

Battn. transferred with Bde. to 25th Div. 18.10.15.

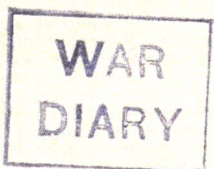

1st BATTN. THE WILTSHIRE REGIMENT.

O C T O B E R

1 9 1 5

Army Form C. 2118.

WAR DIARY
or
INTELLIGENCE SUMMARY.
(Erase heading not required.)

Instructions regarding War Diaries and Intelligence Summaries are contained in F.S. Regs., Part II. and the Staff Manual respectively. Title pages will be prepared in manuscript.

Hour, Date, Place	Summary of Events and Information	Remarks and references to Appendices
October 1st ZILLEBEKE	The Batn relieved 5th LEICESTERS & right of 1st/5th October. A Coy was attached to R.I.R & 5D of B Coy to 2nd S. LANCS; these 2 regts were holding the front line trenches in the new sector taken over by from 138th Brigade. The remainder of the battalion were in dugouts on Railway & Sof ZILLEBEKE and in reserve. Relief completed by 9.30 p.m.	maps
-/- 2nd ZILLEBEKE	Quiet day. Line. The batn were out digging part of the night in Square WOOD & FOSSE WAY e.T.	maps
-/- 3rd ZILLEBEKE	Enemy shelled railway dugouts. Many were blown in. The men were much shaken.	maps

WAR DIARY
or
INTELLIGENCE SUMMARY.
(Erase heading not required.)

Army Form C. 2118.

Hour, Date, Place	Summary of Events and Information	Remarks and references to Appendices
October 3rd ZILLEBEKE	to Culvert & tunnels on the East Bank. No Enemy Casualties. Working parties out during night.	SM
Oct 4th ZILLEBEKE	Fine, Quiet. All available men working at night.	SM
October 5th	Fine - working parties at night. Casualties 1 wounded.	SM
— 6th	Quiet, Fine. 2 Platoons of A Coy returned to ZILLEBEKE. Casualties 1 wounded. A Coy 9th Suffolk Regt. were attached for instruction.	SM
— 7th	Quiet. Remainder of A Coy relieved. The Whole of the Coy returned to dug outs at KRUISTRAAT.	SM

WAR DIARY or INTELLIGENCE SUMMARY.

Army Form C. 2118.

(Erase heading not required.)

Hour, Date, Place	Summary of Events and Information	Remarks and references to Appendices
8th October 15 ZILLEBEKE	Misty day very little shelling. Working parties out at night. no casualties. — A Coy. 7th Suffolks returned to camp; C Coy 7th Suffolks arrived for instruction. —	Nere.
9th " "	Misty day enemy very quiet. — Working parties out at night. At 8.30 p.m enemy whizzbanged the dump this delayed working parties — Parties went out at 8.30 p.m Casualties 2 wounded 1 man 9th Suffolks (attached) killed — 9th Suffolks returned to billets in Fine day.	mons
10th " "	A Coy came up from Kruistraat & took over dugouts. — 2 platoons C Coy sent up to reinforce R.I.R. — Working parties out no casualties a very quiet night. —	mons
11th " "	A very fine morning. Heavy shelling on the left from 8 a.m. to 9.15 a.m. probably at HOOGE ;	

WAR DIARY
or
INTELLIGENCE SUMMARY.
(Erase heading not required.)

Army Form C. 2118.

	Summary of Events and Information	Remarks and references to Appendices
C.B.E.F.	Staugh. 9 pm. Officers 26. O.R. 616. —	
	Previous list " 24 " 563	
	Trench Staugh. " 32 " 426	
	Working parties out at night - no casualties —	MVS
	Very murky morning, but clear by 9.30 a.m. very quiet day. own m.g. fired at german aeroplane. no result. no hostile aeroplanes. patrols out at night. no casualties.	MVS
	June 24. A premature burst from one of our trenches wounded a Sergt. D Coy. enemy railway dugouts in Belwood still showed a marked increase in german trench. four new working parties out at night. B company relieved by a 'head m'tr returning —	MVS
	Misty morning. orders received for relief at night. It has been decided that the Brigade be transferred to Div 23rd 2nd Corps. Bat. relieved by 11th H.L.I. marched East to camp at BUSSEBOOM. Casualties 1 wounded.	COP

WAR DIARY
or
INTELLIGENCE SUMMARY.
(Erase heading not required.)

Army Form C. 2118.

Instructions regarding War Diaries and Intelligence Summaries are contained in F.S. Regs., Part II. and the Staff Manual respectively. Title pages will be prepared in manuscript.

Hour, Date, Place	Summary of Events and Information	Remarks and references to Appendices
October 15th	Quiet & misty. Camp struck & Battalion marched off at 11.30 a.m. to ABEELE. arriving 1.30 p.m.	
16th ABEELE	Quiet & misty. Coys marched to POPERINGHE for baths.	
	Quiet & misty. Battalion was inspected by GEN. HALDANE C.B. D.S.O. at noon. He bid them farewell. The General addressed the Bn. in the following words:—	
17th ABEELE	"Colonel Brown, Officers & N.C.O's and men of the 1st Batt'n Gordon Highrs. I have come to say a few words of farewell on your leaving the 3rd Division. I have no particular reason only the 7th Batt Bn. was drawn this morning to take the senior role, the 7th. I am very sorry to lose you although no doubt you are sorry	

Army Form C. 2118.

WAR DIARY
or
INTELLIGENCE SUMMARY.
(Erase heading not required.)

Instructions regarding War Diaries and Intelligence Summaries are contained in F. S. Regs., Part II. and the Staff Manual respectively. Title pages will be prepared in manuscript.

Hour, Date, Place	Summary of Events and Information	Remarks and references to Appendices
	To leave that "holed ground" HOOGE. I have been with you for eleven months and well remember the first time I met you when you were marching back after that heavy fight round YPRES last November reduced to less than one third of your war strength. Since that time your Battalion has always distinguished itself in fighting work, vigilance and hard soldiering qualities you shewed in the defences of HOOGE when we took over the trenches there you have Look no lighting when any other Batt. in the whole Division. You were at the fighting on the 13th June when we retook SPANBROEK MOLEN and will some of you may remember 16th June, 22nd of June and the 25th of September. On each occasion you distinguished yourselves and proved yourselves a record to the Line. I know I know too well that when the WILTSHIRES were holding the line, that portion of the line was secure establish. I have known command of the 3rd Division so much has not been lost until the other day a small portion in SANCTUARY WOOD was lost, that solely owing to the exhaustion of the troops. Your Battalion has known known than any other Battalion in the Division. I think I am right in saying the...	

(73989) W4141—463. 400,000. 9/14. H.&J.Ltd. Forms/C. 2118/10.

WAR DIARY or INTELLIGENCE SUMMARY

Army Form C. 2118.

Hour, Date, Place	Summary of Events and Information	Remarks and references to Appendices
	Well, goodbye to you all and good luck and I hope from my one day return to the 3rd Division though not necessarily to HOOGE. After the speech the Barclow gave three cheers for General HALDANE and the 3rd Division. General HALDANE then promised the following medals:-	Shorey
	5653 R.S. Maj. S.J. PARKER Medal St George 1st Class	
	1895 Sgt. F. COLLIER " " 3rd "	
	7785 Sgt. A. BULL Distinguished Conduct Medal	NMB
18th October BAILLEUL.	The Bn. left at 5 p.m. & marched to BAILLEUL arriving there at 7.40 p.m. & going into billets. The 3rd Division band was sent to play the Bn. away & played "Auld Lang Syne" etc. — Fine & cold. Company route marches. Lt. Col. E. T. BEEL left the Regiment, to join 2nd in a native Pioneer Corps in MADRAS as 2nd in command. — He had served continuously at the front with the Bn. for 8 months, during the last four months as adjutant.	NMB

WAR DIARY
or
INTELLIGENCE SUMMARY.

(Erase heading not required.)

Army Form C. 2118.

Hour, Date, Place 1915	Summary of Events and Information	Remarks and references to Appendices
19th October BAILLEUL	Fine day. — Battalion Drill. New M.G. class & bombing class. — The Bn. bathed in afternoon. Captain S.S. OGILVIE took over the duties of Acting Adjutant to the Bn.	
20th —"— —"—	Fine day. Bn. Drill. —	
21st —"— —"—	The Bn. was inspected by Sir Charles Ferguson C[in] C 2nd Corps at 9.30 a.m., he welcomed the Bn. back to his Corps, & urged attention to discipline, & appearance of the enemy. — Bn. then went for a route march —	
22nd —"— —"—	Fine days. Bn. drill, & bayonet exercise carried out. —	
23rd —"— —"—		
24th —"— PAPOT	Bn. left BAILLEUL at 9.15 a.m. & marched to PAPOT, where it went into barns, huts, & tents. 2.m. Gmo were sent into the line under command of 2nd Lt 28 Palmer. — Rain in afternoon — Voluntary Church Service at 4.30 m. — Rev. Hickenson joined the Bn. today as Chaplain	

WAR DIARY
or
INTELLIGENCE SUMMARY.

(Erase heading not required.)

Army Form C. 2118.

Hour, Date, Place	Summary of Events and Information	Remarks and references to Appendices
25/15. 6th Nov 1915. PAP07.	Heavy Rain. Working parties for the day cancelled. Short Route March & quick time in afternoon.	S.S. Osthus
26th	Fine day. Baths, Drill and Bayonet Exercises in the morning. M.O. (Capt Lt Hughes) lectures to 8 & D Coys on Bandaging and Field Dressing. Casualties 3 machine gunners wounded, M. Gems wire in the line. —	S.S.O.
27th	Capt. Holles - 2nd Lt Taylor - R.S.M. Parker and 60 other ranks attended a ceremonial Parade before H.M. The King at Bailleul. Remainder of Battalion marched 5 miles to Bruay — went up for working in the trenches. Weather was very wet — much rain.	S.S.O.
28th 29th	PART Wet & showery. Whole battalion and a working party in the trenches — and engaged in putting up huts in the camp.	S.S.O.

Army Form C. 2118.

WAR DIARY
or
INTELLIGENCE SUMMARY.
(Erase heading not required.)

Instructions regarding War Diaries and Intelligence Summaries are contained in F.S. Regs., Part II. and the Staff Manual respectively. Title pages will be prepared in manuscript.

Hour, Date, Place	Summary of Events and Information	Remarks and references to Appendices
30th October 1915 PAPOT	Weather fine. Machine gun and bombing classes otherwise Battalion engaged in working parties in the trenches or hutting in the Camp. Casualties Free issue of beer was made to the Battalion in the evening.	Pte Mahony killed in working party. G.S.O.
31st October -15	Sunday. Church service held by Revd. L.G. Dickinson from Dornhem, who has just been appointed Chaplain to the Regt. & accompanies it to the trenches.	MD

N.F. Brown Lt Colonel
O/C 1/5 Wilts. Regt.

www.ingramcontent.com/pod-product-compliance
Lightning Source LLC
Chambersburg PA
CBHW081403160426
43193CB00013B/2098